MANAGING
BUSINESS
WITH

7

KEY NUMBERS

MANAGING YOUR
BUSINESS
WITH
7
KEY NUMBERS

JEFFREY KENNETH PRAGER
AND SCOTT STROUD

NAHB BuilderBooks.com

National
Association
of Home
Builders

Managing Your Business with 7 Key Numbers

BuilderBooks, a Service of the National Association of Home Builders

Elizabeth M. Rich	Director, Book Publishing
Jena Roach	Book Editor
Jesus Cordero	Cover Design
Electronic Quill Publishing Services	Composition
King Printing Company, Inc.	Printing

Gerald M. Howard NAHB Chief Executive Officer
Lakisha Woods, CAE NAHB Vice President, Publishing & Affinity Programs

Disclaimer

This publication provides accurate information on the subject matter covered. The publisher is selling it with the understanding that the publisher is not providing legal, accounting, or other professional service. If you need legal advice or other expert assistance, obtain the services of a qualified professional experienced in the subject matter involved. The NAHB has used commercially reasonable efforts to ensure that the contents of this volume are complete and appear without error; however the NAHB makes no representations or warranties regarding the accuracy and completeness of this document's contents. The NAHB specifically disclaims any implied warranties of merchantability or fitness for a particular purpose. The NAHB shall not be liable for any loss of profit or any other commercial damages, including but not limited to incidental, special, consequential or other damages. Reference herein to any specific commercial products, process, or service by trade name, trademark, manufacturer, or otherwise does not necessarily constitute or imply its endorsement, recommendation, or favored status by the NAHB. The views and opinions of the author expressed in this publication do not necessarily state or reflect those of the NAHB, and they shall not be used to advertise or endorse a product.

Printed in the United States of America.

18 17 16 15   1 2 3 4 5

ISBN: 978-0-86718-735-9
eISBN: 978-0-86718-736-6

Library of Congress CIP information available on request.

For further information, please contact:

National Association of Home Builders
1201 15th Street, NW
Washington, DC 20005-2800
800-223-2665
Visit us online at BuilderBooks.com

Contents

Figures

Tables

About the Authors

Jeff Prager is the Founder of Backroom Management Services. Backroom provides financial management (accounting, bookkeeping and consulting) services with an emphasis on the construction industry. We use CASHFLO™ which is our own proprietary web-based system that includes a robust accounting, estimating, scheduling and job-costing system. Our focus is on management and growth. Our goal is to help you drive consistent and predictable cash flow.

Jeff has been a CPA, business owner and entrepreneur for over 35 years. He has been a former CEO/CFO and owner of several successful multimillion-dollar companies. He was one of the founders of Ashworth Golf Clothing, the CFO/partner of a large land development company and the owner of Strauss Homes, which was once rated as the second largest privately owned home builder in Colorado and in the top 100 privately owned companies of Colorado (2003). During his career, he has helped companies raise over $1 billion (of which $200 million was for his own companies). Jeff also served as an instructor of managerial economics (applying economic theory to business decisions) at the University of Colorado at Denver.

Scott Stroud has been involved in marketing, designing, selling, and building homes since 1980, when he founded what became an award-winning new home sales company in his home town of Louisville, KY. In 1993, Scott was appointed Vice President of Marketing and Sales for Jim Barna Log Systems. Over the next 10 years, he helped that company increase its sales from $6 million to over $32 million in annual revenues. He has since worked with sales and marketing organizations within the housing industry.

Stroud is the host of BuilderRadio, a popular sales and marketing podcast for builders and Realtors. He is a nationally-known speaker at housing events, an author and a regular contributor to housing journals and blogs.

As Business Development Manager for Power Marketing, a major focus today is in the use of technology as a marketing and sales tool to better attract, capture, and convert leads, particularly online, into the sales funnel. Stroud is an Infusionsoft Certified Partner and helps sales organizations create campaigns that develop more sales, more quickly.

Preface

What is the primary objective of every business owner? Generate profit and, even more importantly, create a positive cash flow. Without cash flow, you can't pay your employees, invest in sales and *marketing*, or grow your *business*.

Let's start with a very simple definition. *Cash flow engineering* is a process to ensure consistent and predictable cash flow. It integrates information, strategies, and automation in the three main areas of your business to drive cash flow.

In cash flow engineering, you view every dollar you spend as an investment. And, if you pay out a dollar, you should get a return of something over and above the dollar you invest. So, in our environment, every dollar you spend on labor is an investment and must return the investment plus a percentage on that investment. That's what cash flow engineering provides—a profit on every dollar that you spend. Cash flow engineering is a process, just like painting a picture by the numbers. Profit isn't a result; it's a plan.

Key Disciplines

In every business there are *three key disciplines:* sales and marketing, operations, and finance. As the owner of a business, how would you know if each facet is successful? How do you determine if your operations department is thriving? How do you know if sales and marketing are succeeding? Finally, how do you know if the financial side of your business is performing, as it should? Please note that there is a huge difference finance and accounting. Finance is not just about your *financial statements*. It is about monitoring and managing your financial and non-financial numbers, creating *cash flow projections*, having the right funds available when you need them and making sure that all aspects of the business are working together to drive cash flow and profit.

Successful companies have people who take responsibility for all three key areas of their business. However, those are the exceptions. Most businesses, even profitable ones, fail to perform as they could or should. Why? The owners or senior managers might play a key role in operations and sales and marketing, but might, for example, leave a void in terms of *financial management*. Your business makes money in *all three areas*. If any one of them is weak, it brings down the total profit potential of the enterprise by as much as one-third.

Don't be confused! Experience, information, and the correct tools are key components of success in all of these areas. Combined, they drive consistent and predictable cash flow.

The entire point of the above conversation—and, in fact, this book—is to demonstrate how each area of your business has a profit opportunity if it is managed according to proven principles that we'll share with you. Particularly with construction companies, the hardest part of running the business is the financial side of it. Finance is generally the area in which the managers and owners have the least amount of experience or knowledge, especially when it comes to understanding how to make money from the financial side of the business! Because it is so misunderstood, most business owners tend to avoid it to their peril. Conversely, the most successful businessmen know how to gain intelligence from their numbers; they make those numbers work *for* them to generate cash flow and profit.

Most of us are used to looking at our businesses in terms of numbers. The purpose of this book is to focus on the *right* numbers; this will help you recognize both problems and opportunities before they become critical so you'll have time to take the appropriate actions. As you proceed through this book, you'll realize that you probably know more than you think. At the same time, other opportunities to increase your cash flow may present themselves to you.

Why don't you monitor your numbers?

One of the most prevalent illnesses business owners have is *Arithmophobia*, the fear of numbers. After all, numbers evoke fear. And the number one symptom of

Arithmophobia is lack of cash: cash to pay yourself, invest in marketing and sales, or reinvest in your business to get it to the size and value you need to adequately compensate you for the risk you take. A lot of business owners run their businesses to survive. There are a few problems with that:

- You're always chasing the next deal.
- Your marketing is disjointed (on again - off again, spray-and-pray).
- You lack confidence that your *business plan* will bring a surplus of customers and the commensurate cash flow and profits.

By the way, we've been there. Running a business this way is a drain of time, energy, and money! In order to run a business, you need to know where you've been, where you are, and where you are going. Whether measuring marketing effort, sales, conversions, *customer retention*, or a host of other bellwether indicators, you need to know your numbers. Our objective is to help you monitor your business and keep it simple by watching your most critical numbers.

Counting beans versus making money!

I pride myself on not being a typical CPA. That's because early in my career, I realized that most businesses hired accountants simply to count the beans to see how much to pay the government. I succeeded by taking a different approach: I would try and look at different businesses in the same market with the same resources and determine why one was successful and the other a failure.

I unlocked the secret by looking in the numbers they tracked and how they used their numbers. To my surprise, it wasn't just the numbers in the financial statements as much as it was in the way they monitored cash and the key factors in their business that drove positive cash flow. Not *all* the numbers, just the seven that make the most difference. Those *7 Key Numbers* drive your whole business funnel and your cash flow, and we'll share them with you in this book.

Think about this: if your business were an NFL team, you would come to game day with your game plan. It's detailed, and each player has his assignments. It's also situational; if something changes, you have to adjust the game plan. That's what the 7 Key Numbers do for you. By following these 7 numbers, you will be able to develop strategies to bridge the gap between where you are today and where you want to be. Starting in Chapter 2, we'll give you a detailed explanation of how to use the 7 Key Numbers and then we'll help you develop strategies to improve them. The objective of this book is to give you the tools you need to become a resounding success.

Imagine

In your mind, project yourself forward 10 years from now. Imagine that you've been running your business successfully for 10 years. Imagine all the skills and knowledge you have gained about your industry, your specialization, your markets, your customers, your competition, and how to maneuver in the business world. Then, imagine being able to come back to today with all that knowledge and experience to apply to your business now. Do you think your business would be any different?

What if you could tap into the mind and experience of someone who had gone down a successful business path for 40 years? Do you think that could help your business? Why? Because running a business is a learned skill! And the key to running a great business is to know your numbers. At the end of the day, you have to know how to track your numbers. You have to know what to look for, when to look for it, and how to use the information so that you can win. These are all skills that you must have to be successful, but few of us start out with them.

When I started I didn't have any of the skills that we'll discuss in this book, yet I went on to own one of the top 100 privately owned companies in Colorado. What we've learned over the past 40 years is the process that can make any business successful. So, you could say that it's taken 40 years to write this book. Those lessons and experiences we share with you on the following pages so that, hopefully, you can learn them much more quickly.

Acknowledgments

We would like to acknowledge that some of the material for this book is from workbooks and materials provided at Backroom Management Services, LLC, as well as from current workshops and seminars being conducted around the country. In addition, we owe a great deal of thanks to David Prager (yes, my son) who helped organize and develop some of this material, Nate Silverman for his helpful insights, and the staff at NAHB who edited this material. Of course, this book wouldn't be in front of you without the help of my friend and associate, Scott Stroud. In my mind, he is the ultimate master of words.

Thanks goes to Mike Krumenacker our illustrator who brought "Bradley" (our company mascot) to life. And finally, I'd like to thank my wife of 43 years (yes, the best 43 years of my life) for her willingness to let me work on this book during our evenings and weekends.

—Jeff Prager

I, too, must acknowledge the mentors and influencers that have had an impact on my life and understanding of new-home marketing. This list must include all the industry professionals who have allowed me to interview them for BuilderRadio and have openly shared their wisdom with all of us. Most notable, though, and among the most powerful influences on my teaching and career are the late Jerry Rouleau, who accepted me as a partner and friend;

Brian Flook, with whom I continue to share a close relationship and deep gratitude; my incredibly patient and understanding wife of 37 years, Melanie, and my co-author, Jeff Prager, who has awakened my left brain and taught me the value of watching these numbers. May this book help you to do the same.

—**Scott Stroud**

Introduction

If the number one symptom of Arithmophobia is lack of cash, what's the cure? Get an accounting degree? Absolutely not! Here's a deep dark secret your accountant won't tell you: all you need to understand your numbers and to run your business better is two things. First, just simple third-grade math. Nothing fancy, just basic addition, subtraction, multiplication, and division. Even better? Computers can do most of it for you! Second, you need to have the ability to point your thumbs. Point your thumbs up if things are on track or better than expected. Thumbs down if things aren't what you expected or worse than you expected. Are sales what you expected? Are costs within reason? Thumbs up or thumbs down?

This book will explain how you can interpret your accounting data to grow your business—even if you suffer from Arithmophobia. Numbers can be both a lagging indicator (like your financial statements, which tell you what you should already know) and your leading indicators, which tell you where you're going. We also hope to illustrate how you can improve your ability to use these numbers to make it easier for others (management, investors, and creditors) to judge your operations, your probable future, and operating results so they can assist you. We are not attempting to cover the whole range of financial analysis or projections, but we limited our discussions to basic financial planning and creditor relations.

This book is not just about numbers. It is about cash flow engineering: developing systems and processes to ensure consistent and predictable cash flow.

"A problem is a problem until you reduce it to a procedure," is a saying I constantly use. By spending time at the front end, you will save hours and hours of time at the back end. Why? Because you won't fall into the trap that ensnares most entrepreneurs and business owners—reinventing the wheel every time you do a job!

In this book, we will share with you many of our "wheels"—proven procedures that we've developed and refined over the years that will enable you to create the results you want.

Problems in Growth

The building industry is characterized by many small- to medium-size operators with a high degree of changing management and a changing legal and regulatory environment. This translates into high risk and an uncertain future.

Cash is our number one concern, and we need this cash in order to grow. This is true with all companies, but is especially important in uncertain environments just to survive, let alone grow.

Of course, growth has its own challenges. Just on the financial side, rapid growth creates a need for more capital to support that growth. You often need more front-end money to allow for larger volume. Yet, turnover ratios tend to decline. So, the question is: Where do we begin?

Three Basic Functions in a Business

There are three basic functions in a business: sales and marketing, operations and financial management.

It's hard enough for a business owner to be great at all three functions, and few businesses have the luxury of having specialists to perform each well. So, for an owner to succeed at all three as an individual, he may need a little help. That is the purpose of this book. In particular, we are going to elaborate on all three functions through three simple yet powerful concepts: The 7 Key Numbers help manage daily cash flow through your entire sales and marketing (and business) funnel and the *5 C's of financial management* are designed to continually sharpen and refine your business processes.

Some of this discussion parallels topics that were discussed in *The Peddler's Son: How my Dad's Tiny Business Taught Me to Grow Multimillion-Dollar Companies* by Jeffrey Kenneth Prager. The *Peddler's Son* focuses on the six long-term success factors. The key word is *long-term*. In the short term, you need to focus on the 7 Key Numbers that drive business success. We will learn how to use those 7 Key Numbers and determine which ones we like and which ones we dislike. Based on that, we will develop strategies to improve those numbers. All 7 Key Numbers will have an influence on the profits you make, so we will look at each one individually.

As an aside, I am an economist by training. Why is that important? Because, as an economist, we focus on the short term, the intermediate term, and the long term. As a CPA, I was taught to look only one year into the future. That's maybe what's wrong with Wall Street as well.

Why Do You Need Numbers?

Over my life, I've thought about this a lot, and as I've worked for companies, or as I've run my own businesses, I've noticed that those who succeed never think in terms of pennies. In fact, they do something that most people running a business don't: *they manage their numbers.* So, let's look at why you need better numbers:

- **To manage the business.** This includes planning, organizing, directing, and monitoring all aspects of the business.
- **To expand the business.** A business can't expand without proper preparation and planning. In order to expand, you need to understand the investment you are going to make, the cost of the expansion, and have a plan for getting the capital to achieve your goal.
- **To sell the business.** If you eventually want to sell your business, a prospective purchaser will probably look at historical financial statements as a *benchmark* for future performance. If the financial statements are not representative of actual past performance, they could delay or even sabotage your deal. One thing we consistently hear from business brokers is that they can't really maximize the value of a business because they don't have good numbers.
- **To raise capital.** Without the right numbers and the right plans in place, you can't raise the necessary money to fund the business's growth. Banks tell us that the biggest impediment to lending is the financial state of the business.
- **To lower taxes.** How would you like to pay no taxes? My goal is to pay $1 million in taxes. Think about what I just said. What does it mean if I pay $1 million in taxes? It means I'm making *a lot* of money. So don't let the tail wag the dog. Make your economic deal then structure that deal to minimize your tax liability.

Is Your Business Where You Want It?

Let's start by taking a short quiz. This survey allows you to rate the vital components of your company. It also helps you prioritize and develop a game plan for improving your company and achieving your goals. For each question, rate yourself on a scale from 1 to 10.

---

1. Are you satisfied with your cash flow and profit?   1 2 3 4 5 6 7 8 9 10
In evaluating this question, think about the following: Least satisfied   Most satisfied

- Are you meeting the profit goals you established for your business?
- Do you have predictable cash flow?
- Are you worried about making payroll?
- Do you have the resources you need to achieve your goals?

2. Are you satisfied with your productivity?   1 2 3 4 5 6 7 8 9 10
In evaluating this question, think about the following: Least satisfied   Most satisfied

- Are you spending most of your time on your core talent? Or are you occupied with a lot of administrative tasks?
- Do you have a clear picture as to which products and customers are making you money?
- Can you identify which salespeople are performing?
- Can you identify which marketing efforts are succeeding?
- Are you able to use up-to-date numbers to make financial decisions to run your business?
- Are you reluctant to accept new technologies and processes?

3. Are you satisfied with your growth?   1 2 3 4 5 6 7 8 9 10
In evaluating this question, think about the following: Least satisfied   Most satisfied

- Are you achieving consistent growth?
- Do you have a consistent supply of new leads?
- Do you know which lead sources deliver and who follows them up?
- Are you getting repeat business from existing customers?

4. Are you satisfied with your lifestyle?   1 2 3 4 5 6 7 8 9 10
In evaluating this question, think about the following: Least satisfied   Most satisfied

- Are you reaching the goals you had envisioned when you started?
- Are you enjoying the business?
- Are you on target to exit your business? That is, are you building wealth in your business?
- Are you earning what you expected when you started the business?
- Do you have the time you want to spend with friends and family?
- Are you in control? Or do you feel at the mercy of your bookkeeper?

Overall assessment: _____ **out of 40**

If your score is between 35 and 40, congratulations! You have a good handle on managing the key elements of your business. If your score is between 30 and 35, then some tune-up work will make you more effective. If your score is under 30, then you might want to stop and assess your internal processes. And if your score is under 25, then "Houston, we have a problem!"

In any case, this assessment may be either a formality to clear your thinking or truly transformational.

Definition of a Business

A business is a well-positioned, well-defined organization generating cash flow that encourages growth and leads to building wealth. The key to this definition is that the company is *organized*. The company management understands its internal and external strengths, weaknesses, opportunities, and threats (or what we call SWOT).

Well-positioned is an external definition (based on the customers' point of view) that means the company clearly understands its mission, vision, products, and target market. It understands which trends in the competitive environment might be threats and which might be opportunities. It means understanding the price, targeting the right client with the right message. Leverage the business's position to its advantage.

Well-defined is an internal definition that means the company has well-developed, well-implemented methods and systems for production, distribution, pricing, accounting, financial management, human resources, etc. A well-defined business grows in profitability. It has methods and systems in place to produce a consistent customer and employee experience. It consistently produces and sells quality products. The company is also well managed. When it makes a mistake, it not only corrects the mistake but improves the flaws in the system that led to that decision. It learns from the experience.

Compensation to an Owner

When you own a business, you must make money as an owner and as an investor. Most businesses are designed to create an environment to pay the owner a salary. In reality, most don't even cover the salary an owner would make by having a job, let alone compensate him for his sweat equity—the feeling of waking up at three in the morning in a cold sweat, wondering how to make tomorrow's payroll. As a business owner, you need to be compensated for your sweat equity.

As a business owner, you should plan on getting paid in three different ways:

- First, you should budget your *fixed costs* to include a yearly salary that, at a minimum, would equal the amount you'd receive doing the same work for someone else.
- Second, you should budget a profit goal to compensate you for the risk, the sweat, and the stress you endure as a business owner.
- Finally, you should get paid for the value you created when you reach your long-term goals. At that point, you can either sell your business, go public, or double down to build an even bigger business.

Types of Business Owners

There are two types of business owners: shopkeepers and successful business owners. The shopkeeper is an individual who opens his store at eight in the morning, closes at five, and goes to his accountant around April 15th and asks him how much was left over. When the shopkeeper makes money, it's a pleasant surprise. This owner is just surviving.

As we said before, there are problems in just surviving. If your objective is to just survive then you probably aren't running your business for the long term. Ironically, this makes it much tougher to survive in the short term too. For example, you are probably always chasing the next deal, at least it feels that way. You likely also have disjointed marketing; it isn't a system that keeps the pipeline full month after month, year after year. In the end, it's almost a chicken-and-egg situation. If you want to just survive, it's a safe bet that you don't have the necessary confidence that will get the business to the next level generating the required cash flow and profits you need. Does the lack of confidence drive the objective to survive or does the short-sighted objective create the lack of confidence? In either case, you are right.

Conversely, the successful business owner performs an ongoing analysis of how the business is doing and what he or she might do to improve its performance. When this business owner makes money, it's the predictable result of executing a well-considered plan.

So, which do you want to be? You do have a choice. You could earn money both as an employee or as an investor, but you must transition from a passive business owner who lets time control you, to a successful business owner where you control your own fate.

You are a business owner, and as a business owner, you just have three resources:

- Time, which refers to *your time only*. It does not include your employees' time, which you pay for as money.
- Energy, which accounts for your effort, frustration, mental expenditure, and emotional engagement with your business.
- Money can be separated into labor and non-labor costs, like materials and supplies.

Now, which one provides *your* competitive advantage? Do you have a competitive advantage when it comes to money? Probably not! There are always businesses with deeper pockets. And if it just comes to money, your business would always lose.

Is your competitive advantage that you do everything yourself, assuming that hard work and long hours are necessary for success? Here's the reality: Working 10-hour days onsite, then spending your evenings doing paperwork and accounting until the wee hours are not a way to earn money. That's a recipe for saving money but not making money. You need systems and a process that gives you more time, energy, and money . . . and that's the purpose of this book! We want to give you a system for generating a lucrative business. Our goal in this book is to help you generate more cash flow now, institute change that maximizes cash flow, and finally turn your business into a cash cow, creating long-term value.

1

The 7 Key Numbers that Drive Revenue and Cash Flow

The 5 C's of Financial Management

Let's take a step back and talk about management in general. The 5 C's are the key to management of every aspect of your business (fig 1.1). They relate to your action plan and represent a proactive philosophy designed to continually sharpen and refine every one of your business processes.

Here are the 5 C's:

- **Create your benchmarks.** Also called key performance indicators, these benchmarks will be used to measure the progress of your business. Using the 7 Key Numbers and strategically aligning them with your goals create these benchmarks.
- **Collect meaningful information.** This includes both financial and non-financial information. You need this to track your progress toward your goals.
- **Compile your data.** Information is worthless in its raw form. This step puts it in a format that's easy to understand, interpret, and act upon.
- **Compare your results.** Place your compiled data side-by-side with the benchmarks you created in the first C. And then . . .
- **Correct your trajectory.** Take the corrective steps necessary to get closer to your goals.

In high school science, you used the scientific method. Briefly stated, it says create a hypothesis (create a benchmark), test the hypothesis (collect data), compile the data,

FIGURE 1.1 The 5 C's of financial management

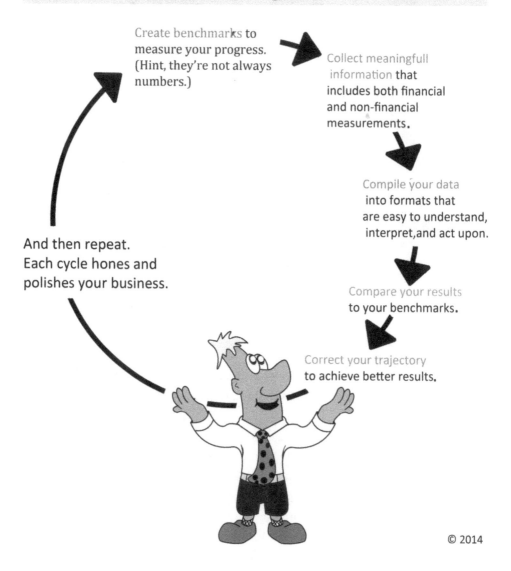

Create benchmarks to measure your progress. (Hint, they're not always numbers.)

Collect meaningfull information that includes both financial and non-financial measurements.

Compile your data into formats that are easy to understand, interpret, and act upon.

And then repeat. Each cycle hones and polishes your business.

Compare your results to your benchmarks.

Correct your trajectory to achieve better results.

© 2014

compare the data to your hypothesis, and finally form a conclusion. Do you see the similarity? This system has been around for generations, and it still works.

We are going to use the first of the 5 C's to define your 7 Key Numbers—creating a benchmark. The 7 Key Numbers are designed to create the expectations for performance of your company as a whole. Later on, we can break these numbers down into specific performance goals of your company. In Chapter 6 we will go into detail about the remaining four C's and show how you can use them to manage all aspects of our business.

7 Key Numbers That Drive Your Business

Ask yourself a simple question: exactly how many *leads* do you need to generate this year to make your profit goal? Specifically, what is your profit goal? In just 7 steps, you can go from abstract goals to tangible benchmarks you need to meet your goals! Yes, it is that easy.

As business owners, there are lots of numbers that we have to look at every day. But the numbers in your financial statements don't tell you the whole story. You need to make running your business simpler and that can be accomplished by distilling all your figures, ratios, and reports into just 7 Key Numbers. These 7 numbers drive all revenue and profits. If you learn to manage these 7 numbers, you'll be able to manage your sales, your growth, and your business's future!

In most business information systems, you look at your financial statements to see how your business activities generate profit. But there's another way to do it. Decide how much profit you want to make, and then adjust your business activities to reach that goal.

Figure 1.2 explains what we call the *perfect cash flow cycle,* which is explained in terms of the 7 Key Numbers. It starts with leads and ends with cash in the bank.

FIGURE 1.2 The perfect cash flow cycle

© 2014

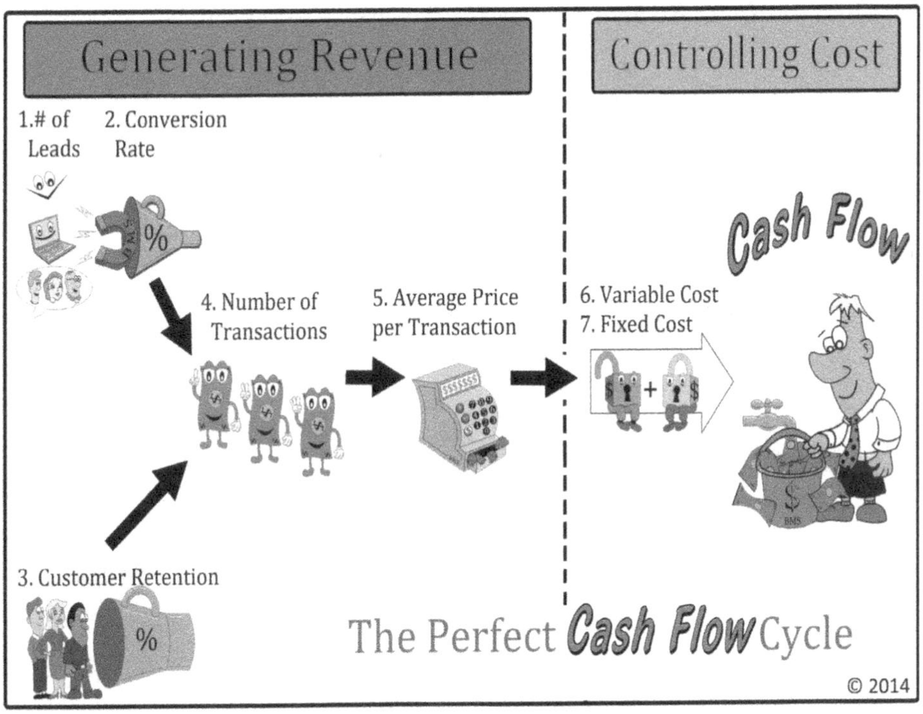

As an overview, you can generate sales from two sources: new leads or existing clients. You start by attracting leads. And through a *lead magnet*—an offering, an *elevator speech,* or something that grabs attention—you nurture and convert that lead into a sale. So, the first number is the lead generation, and the second number is the *conversion rate.* How many people do you have to talk to in order to garner a sale?

The third number is customer retention. Customer retention starts with product fulfillment, satisfaction, and service; it develops into a full customer journey. Note that the sales conversion funnel is smaller than the customer-retention funnel (as expected) to keep a greater percentage of customers coming back, *upsell* them, and/or get referrals from them.

The fourth is the number of transactions per customer, and that is reinforced through customer support, lifetime value, and *referral sales.* The fifth number is your *average price per transaction;* this discussion includes price, incentives, premiums, and terms of the sale. Notice again that the first five numbers generate revenue. The last two control costs.

The sixth and seventh numbers measure your *variable costs* and your fixed costs, respectively. Variable costs are the costs of production, delivery, fulfillment, and follow-up. Fixed costs are the costs of keeping your doors open, whether you make sales or not.

Whatever is left over is cash flow for you to use to pay yourself and your employees more, invest in marketing and sales, or reinvest in your business.

The 7 Key Numbers Are About Keeping Score

The key to any game is to win, and there is a sequence of steps involved in winning:

- To win, you must keep score.
- To score, you must have a strategy.
- To execute a strategy, you must make good decisions.
- To make good decisions, you need to know the score.

In some ways, business is like a game. To win, you must keep score. Let's take baseball as an example. What is the objective of a baseball game? To score more points than your opposition! To score, you must have a strategy. How do you score more points? By hitting the ball when you are at bat! But to execute a strategy, you need to make good decisions, such as, when to swing, when to let the ball go by you, when to bunt, etc. Simple, right? And how do you know you made a good decision? By measuring the score!

Do you see how it's circular? It all comes back to the need to know where you are at all times.

The 7 Key Numbers tell you the score. Nobody wants to go through their financial statements every single day, which is why the 7 Key Numbers are so powerful. They're like headlines for your business; you glance at them every morning to know what's going to impact you that day.

But, it's not just numbers. . . You need the *right* numbers. Remember, only the 7 Key Numbers are necessary to manage an entire business. These 7 Key Numbers show you exactly where business owners need to invest their time, energy, and money in order to profit.

Five of the seven numbers have nothing to do with accounting—they drive revenues. The other 2 control costs. But what is the lowest you can get your costs to? Zero. And what does that mean? It means you are out of business. Focus on revenue-driving numbers and then start figuring out how you will minimize your costs. Let's list the seven numbers and show what we are measuring. By the way, the key word is "measuring." Why? Because you can only manage what you measure. So here are the seven key numbers:

1. **Number of leads.** For measuring marketing effectiveness
2. **Sales conversion rate.** For measuring sales effectiveness
3. **Customer retention rate.** For driving long-term customer value
4. **Number of transactions per customer.** For driving cash flow and repeat business
5. **Average price per transaction.** For driving cash flow and boosting margins
6. **Variable costs.** For managing production expenditures
7. **Fixed costs.** For managing overhead and efficiencies

Now let's put these into practice.

Creating Expectations

Let's work with a hypothetical company and marry the 5 C's of financial management with the 7 Key Numbers. This example is based on a real company where we utilized this process to turn the company around. As we work with this hypothetical company, insert your numbers next to theirs.

Vandelay is a ten-year-old company in Arvada, Colorado. They're a mom-and-pop operation founded by Art Vandelay with his wife, Susan, handling the books. They have a couple of hourly employees and an administrator to keep track of all their jobs and keep their vans rolling to the right locations.

A couple of years ago, they specialized in basement remodels and their average sale was $10,000. As the economy worsened, they made a decision to do handyman work in order to keep their crews working and their doors open.

Art was struggling, but didn't know what to do. His accountant provided a *balance sheet* and *income statement,* but Art really didn't understand the financial statements nor did he really understand the number that drove his business. In short, he didn't know the *score.*

Knowing he was in trouble, he decided to utilize cash flow engineering to help him diagnose his business. The first thing we did was to layout a seven-step process to begin to understand what was going on. As you may have guessed, this process was all about learning the score.

Step 1. We asked Art to determine the amount of profit he wanted to target as a goal. Art said his profit goal was $30,000, compensation for his sweat equity. We made certain this didn't include his salary. What is your profit goal? Profit is the money you receive after paying all your expenses, including your salary.

Don't think of profit as a four-letter word. Profits are the lifeblood of any company and can allow your business to do any number of things it would be incapable of without them: reduce debt, pay taxes, invest in your people (raises, bonuses, increased benefits, increased training), invest in your company (savings for that rainy day, improved work facilities, expansion of the business), or pay yourself (dividends or pay it forward).

Profits are your compensation for the risk you take and the sleepless nights you endure. They will make your business venture worthwhile and will allow your company to thrive and grow.

Step 2. We then determined Art's fixed costs. In Art's case, it costs him $120,000 per year to keep his doors open. We made certain that Art included his salary as part of these fixed costs as well as his overhead, such as his administrator's salary, rent, utilities, insurance, permits, and so on.

Step 3. Next, we determined his variable costs as a percentage of sales. These costs included the hourly rate for his two workers, the cost of running the vans, and any materials needed to complete the jobs. Because Vandelay had started taking such small jobs, their gross margin was pretty low, averaging about 25% of their sales revenue.

Based on his profit goal and his fixed costs, we know Art needs to generate $600,000 of sales revenue. We'll talk about break-even in a later chapter but basically his profit goal ($30,000) plus fixed costs ($120,000) divided by his *gross profit margin* (25%) is $600,000 (fig. 1.3). Think of it this way: For every sales dollar you generate, you can only use 25 cents for overhead and profit. Kind of scary, isn't it?

FIGURE 1.3 Calculating profit goal

Key Number	Plan
Profit goal	$30,000
7. Fixed costs	$120,000

Total Costs to Cover (Line 1 + Line 2)	$150,000
6. Variable costs	75%
Gross Profit Margin (1- line 4)	25%

Revenue goal (Line 3 ÷ Line 5)	*$600,000*

Step 4. Determine average sales price or revenue per job or transaction. In this case, Vandelay started taking smaller and smaller jobs. As part of their new reactive sales strategy they wouldn't turn down any work whatsoever.

Now, some people may think in terms of dollars or the revenue they need to generate. But the balance of the steps analyze the components that drive revenue. And, these components can be measured and managed. For instance, number of sales, average dollar sales and gross revenues are related. Understanding how many unit sales you need to close each month is actionable and measurable. It is also easy to calculate: sales divided by average price per sale yields the number of units to sell.

At Vandelay, they found they were not being called to remodel a basement nearly as often as they were called to caulk a shower or repair some drywall that a teenager has kicked through. As the years went on and they accepted more and more small jobs, their average revenue per job dropped from $10,000 to $600! Based on his per unit price, we knew that he needed 1,000 sales per year ($600,000 divided by an average price of $600) in order to make his revenue objective (fig 1.4). If you think in terms of two hundred working days per year, that's three jobs a day. They had 2 vans to keep busy, but that's a lot of work!

FIGURE 1.4 Vandelay's annual sales goal

Key Number	Plan
Profit goal	$30,000
7. Fixed costs	$120,000

Total Costs to Cover (Line 1 + Line 2)	$150,000
6. Variable costs	75%
Gross Profit Margin (1- line 4)	25%

Revenue goal (Line 3 ÷ Line 5)	*$600,000*
5. Average price per transaction	$600
Total units sales goal (line 6 ÷ line 7)	1,000

Here's a fact that should not surprise you: Sales come from customers. In most industries, customers buy from you more than once, even in the homebuilding industry, although the sales cycle may be several years between purchases. From a practical standpoint, translating the number of unit sales needed into number of customers related affects your marketing costs, your customer service costs, and your sales approach.

Step 5. Determine the number of transactions per customer. Vandelay had a reputation for superior work in their field. Doing more and more handyman work coupled with their strategy to not turn away any work increased the number of transactions per customer. In fact, they keep a list of their customers, and they send out mailers every so often to keep customers coming back. It seems to work, because their customers tend to call them about four times a year.

So, to sell 1,000 jobs, they need an active client list of 250 customers (1,000 jobs divided by 4 jobs per customer on average) as seen in figure 1.5.

FIGURE 1.5 Number of customers needed to make annual sales goal

Key Number	Plan
Profit goal	$30,000
7. Fixed costs	$120,000

Total Costs to Cover (Line 1 + Line 2)	$150,000
6. Variable costs	75%
Gross Profit Margin (1- line 4)	25%

Revenue goal (Line 3 ÷ Line 5)	$600,000
5. Average price per transaction	$600
Total units sales goal (line 6 ÷ line 7)	1,000
4. Number of transactions per customer	4
Number of Customers Needed (Line 8 ÷ Line 9)	250

What is the cost of generating a new customer? Chances are, it's more than you expect. That's why retaining existing customers is so critical to your profits and cash flow. Additional sales to your customer base don't carry the burden of acquisition cost, and that means more profit for you. Increasing customer retention through proper nurturing may have other impacts on your staffing as well.

Where may you need more staff?   Where may you need fewer staff?

_____   _____

_____   _____

_____   _____

Step 6. Determine the number of existing customers and the retention rate. Over the years, Vandelay has a history of keeping approximately 50% of the customers that he started the year with. Of the 100 customers he had at the beginning of the year, he still does work for 50. They need 250 customers doing an average of 4 jobs per year, so they need to get 200 more customers (250 less the 50 retained). This is illustrated in figure 1.6

FIGURE 1.6 Number of new customers needed

Key Number	Plan
Profit goal	$30,000
7. Fixed costs	$120,000

Total Costs to Cover (Line 1 + Line 2)	$150,000
6. Variable costs	75%
Gross Profit Margin (1- line 4)	25%

Revenue goal (Line 3 ÷ Line 5)	$600,000
5. Average price per transaction	$600
Total units sales goal (line 6 ÷ line 7)	1,000
4. Number of transactions per customer	4
Number of Customers Needed (Line 8 ÷ Line 9)	250
Number of existing customers	100
3. Rate of customer retention	50%

Number of retained customers (line 11 x line 12)	50

Number of new customers needed (line 10 - line 13)	200

How do you attract your customers to begin with? Marketing. Marketing brings leads into your sales pipeline. Understanding how many leads you need helps you determine your marketing *budget* and staffing requirements.

Step 7. Determine the rate at which they convert leads to sales. In terms of sales, the people at Vandelay were not very sophisticated; whoever answered the phone was the salesperson of the moment. So from that respect, they actually lost a lot of business because they don't really have a process for turning leads into customers. As a result, they only converted 1 out of every 4 leads—a 25% conversion rate.

Starting with the profit goal of $30,000 and considering all the information gathered in the other steps, the company needs to generate 800 new leads (200 new customers divided by 25% conversion rate) this year in order to reach their profit goal (fig 1.7).

FIGURE 1.7 Leads target

Key Number	Plan
Profit goal	$30,000
7. Fixed costs	$120,000

Total Costs to Cover (Line 1 + Line 2)	$150,000
6. Variable costs	75%
Gross Profit Margin (1- line 4)	25%

Revenue goal (Line 3 ÷ Line 5)	*$600,000*
5. Average price per transaction	$600
Total units sales goal (line 6 ÷ line 7)	1,000
4. Number of transactions per customer	4
Number of Customers Needed (Line 8 ÷ Line 9)	250
Number of existing customers	100
3. Rate of customer retention	50%

Number of retained customers (line 11 x line 12)	50

Number of new customers needed (line 10 - line 13)	200
2. Conversion rate	25%
	---------
1. Leads target	800

With the analysis now completed, Art now has a pretty good picture of what needs to happen for Vandelay Remodeling to achieve his profit goal. Believe it or not, we actually painted a very specific picture of this company using essentially seven key metrics—The 7 Key Numbers.

Your Corporate Goals—Turn the Equation Upside Down

Now let's look at the funnel the way most people look at it, from leads to profit. This helps you in two ways: you can see the whole funnel from a managerial perspective and assess if this is realistic.

It's worth reiterating that sales revenue was not one of the 7 Key Numbers. In working with Art, we were able to calculate that the company has a sales goal of $600,000, but that shouldn't be his focus. Sales are the result of other activities.

This model is a *proactive* model in that it tells us where we need to be. In building his 7 Key Numbers, we can see that Art needs to focus on the activities that will allow him to generate his sales and profit goals. If Art and his team focus on these key activities and achieve the metrics they planned, then the sales, and ultimately the profits, will be there.

Now that we have created some benchmarks and expectations, we can manage the company and generate an action plan. In figure 1.8, you can see the7 Key Numbers, starting with the 800 leads Vandelay needs to generate. The numbers are the same in the plan we just generated; they're just presented in reverse order. This is how we use them to manage progress toward achieving goals.

FIGURE 1.8 Using the 7 Key Numbers to manage progress toward Vandelay's goals

Key Number	Plan
1. Number of leads generated	800
2. Conversion rate	25%
Number of existing customers	*100*
3. Rate of customer retention	50%
4. Number of transactions per customer	*4*
5. Average price per transaction	**$600**
Number of units sold	1,000
Revenue	*$600,000*
6. Variable costs	75%
7. Fixed costs	$120,000

Profit	*$30,000*

So let's move the clock forward and look at how Art is doing against his plan.

Compare Your Results to Your Targets

The column on the left in figure 1.9 is the plan we created. The column on the right is the company's actual performance. We will compare our actual results to those Art thought were going on or achievable.

FIGURE 1.9 Comparing the plan to actual results

Key Number	Plan	Actual	
1. Number of leads generated	800	500	←
2. Conversion rate	25%	25%	
Number of existing customers	100	100	
3. Rate of customer retention	50%	50%	
4. Number of transactions per customer	4	4	
5. Average price per transaction	$600	$500	←
Number of units sold	1,000	700	
Revenue	$600,000	$350,000	
6. Variable costs	75%	80%	←
7. Fixed costs	$120,000	$120,000	
	--------	--------	
Profit	$30,000	($50,000)	

As you can see, Art had three major weaknesses:

- Lead generation
- Average price per transaction
- Variable costs

Now, we're going to teach you the secret to being an accountant. A number in and of itself has no value. You need a benchmark, a number to which you compare your results. Managing your business is simply comparing two numbers. (Creating your benchmarks is also the first C of financial management.)

For instance, if I said I generated $50,000 in profit this year, is that good or bad? Well, we don't know. But if I said I generated $50,000 in profit and the prior year I did $10,000, would you point your thumbs up or down? Thumbs up! But if I generated $500,000 in profit the prior year, how would you point your thumbs? Thumbs down!

If you have a benchmark, then you can say something is good or bad and requires attention. You don't need to be a mathematician; you just need to be able to point your thumbs *up* or *down*. It seems so simple. But that's really the essence of management: comparing two numbers and deciding which one you like better.

© 2014

One of the reasons the 7 Key Numbers is so powerful is because it creates a framework for reducing complex business problems into simple thumbs-up-or-down decisions. In our example, to generate leads, Vandelay relies primarily on neighborhood flyers and door hangers as well as Google ads and the Yellow Pages. Using these marketing tools, their goal was to create 800 leads, but they only got 500. Thumbs up or thumbs down? Thumbs down!

As we mentioned earlier, Vandelay had no formal sales process, sales training or people assigned to sales. In fact, as we said before, whoever answered the phone was the sales person. On average, they closed 25% of the leads they generated.

They had 100 existing clients at the beginning of the year and kept about 50% active during the year. On average, they closed 4 jobs per customer at an average price of $500 per job. As a result of their performance on these key activities, they only made 700 sales as opposed to their goal of 1,000 and only generated $350,000 in gross revenue compared to their goal of $600,000. Thumbs up or thumbs down?

In addition to coming up short on their revenue, their profit margins are being squeezed because of the lower prices they are charging to get business and the high costs of sending their vans all over the town. Remember, their target for variable costs was 75% of sales, which would have generated a 25% gross margin. Instead, their costs have risen to 80% of sales, generating a 20% gross-profit margin. That means for every dollar they earn, 80% of it goes to cover the cost of producing the unit, leaving only 20% to cover their fixed costs and profit.

You've probably guessed that things aren't looking good. Do you think that Vandelay is going to generate a profit? In fact, they are on target to lose $50,000. Guess where that money comes from? You guessed it. It comes directly out of the owner's salary. Obviously, this is not a sustainable situation.

As you can see, they are not reaching their leads goal or their average price per transaction goal, and they are not controlling their variable costs.

By focusing on the 7 Key Numbers, management can react *before* the situation becomes a disaster. As an analogy let's look at how we read *The Wall Street Journal*. The paper is jammed with information, which is generally far more than we need or have time to read, let alone process. We rely on the headlines to know at a glance what's going to impact our business today.

The 7 Key Numbers are like the headlines for your business. They simplify management by showing you what you need to pay attention to today. Believe it or not, these 7 Key Numbers are everything you need to manage your business.

Develop Strategies to Get Your Numbers on Track

So, what can we do? Well, let's determine what changes can be made to get Vandelay back on track. We've used the 7 Key Numbers to build his plan, and we've compared his results to see where he is. Now, let's ask what we can change in the short term to at least get him profitable.

One of the first places to look is sales or, more specifically, key activities that generate sales. We know that Art doesn't have much money to invest in marketing, but in talking with Art we agree that his sales process needs to be more formalized. Without much effort, he can ask his team to stop trying to handle every call themselves. They could create a fact-finding sheet to identify the needs of their prospect and give it to Art so that he could follow up and close the sales loop. As it turns out, Art has a real talent for working with customers to develop rapport, build trust, and close a sale. By leveraging this, they believe they will be able to increase their closing rate from 25% to 35%.

In the short run, there wasn't much he could do about customers, customer retention, and number of transactions per customer, but in addition to generating more customers, the *dashboard* is suggesting that they should look at how they could increase the average price they get on each job.

After some discussion with Art and his team, we decided that by becoming more selective as to what jobs they took, they could go after more jobs that allowed them to focus on their skills and services as opposed to price. By doing this they will be able to increase the average price per job from $500 to $750. (As an aside, we let his competitors do the smaller jobs. Why? Because they couldn't even break even on these jobs. Why pay your customers to do their work?)

As a result of just these two changes—improving the sales process to close more sales and increasing the average price per job—Art and his team should be able to dramatically improve Vandelay Remolding's situation.

If they execute their new strategy and keep focused on the numbers, they can improve their number of units sold to 900 and increase their revenue from $350,000 to $675,000 without even increasing the number of leads they generate.

Figure 1.10 shows that with a little change we can generate $15,000 in profit. While they are short of Art's profit goal of $30,000, these changes will significantly change the trajectory of the company. As they continue to focus on their 7 Key Numbers and work to improve their variable costs, they should be able to hit their target.

FIGURE 1.10 Small changes to the plan can change the company's trajectory

Key Number	Plan	Actual	Focus
1. Number of leads generated	800	500	500
2. Conversion rate	25%	25%	35%
Number of existing customers	100	100	100
3. Rate of customer retention	50%	50%	50%
4. Number of transactions per customer	4	4	4
5. Average price per transaction	$600	$500	$750
Number of units sold	1,000	700	900
Revenue	$600,000	$350,000	$675,000
6. Variable costs	75%	80%	80%
7. Fixed costs	$120,000	$120,000	$120,000
Profit	$30,000	($50,000)	$15,000

This is the essence of the 7 Key Numbers and how to use them to improve your business management and, in turn, your results. Now, this was the quick Band-Aid fix.

This a system for not only identifying problem areas, but for improving business performance, month after month, year after year. Remember, one of the value drivers in the ultimate sale of your business will be consistency of earnings. You can use the 7 Key Numbers as a tool to plan for retirement, sale of the business, additional financing, and a host of other planning activities.

Now it's your turn. Start with your profit goals and create a spreadsheet (or even do it on the back of a napkin!) to work your 7 Key Numbers. Your goal is to create a business that not only pays you a salary, but allows you to grow your business to the size and value you need to generate the cash flow and lifestyle you deserve. These 7 Key Numbers are your secret weapon and the keys to the kingdom.

Using the 7 Numbers to Create Your Operating Budget

Budgeting is basically a projected income statement that quantifies the objectives and expectations of all units of an organization. For example, you may want to budget your costs for sales, production, and finance. Budgeting is a process of estimating revenues and expenses before they occur.

These functions are served by a budget:

- Compel management planning
- Evaluating performance, based on expectations
- Coordinating activities in terms of operating decisions
- Helps implement plans
- Promotes communication and coordination among the various segments of a business.
- The ultimate objective of a business is to create long-term, positive cash flow through operations.
- Negative cash flow—Money goes out of your pocket faster than you can put it in your pocket.
- Break-even cash flow—Money goes out of your pocket at the same rate as it enters your pocket.
- Positive cash flow—Money goes into your pocket faster than it goes out leaving money for you!

The purpose of this chapter was to expose you to the framework of the 7 Key Numbers for analyzing a business. Once you get good at this you can do it on the back of a napkin (simplicity is always the ultimate tool to understand anything). When analyzing a new project, a new strategy, a new program, pencil out your expectations in the 7-number framework. This will become a key to analyzing every aspect of your company.

In the following chapters, we will go into more detail on each of the 7 Key Numbers.

2

Generating Leads (#1 of 7)

The first of the 7 Key Numbers we measure is the number of new leads or sales opportunities coming into your business. You can get new leads from a number of sources— word of mouth referrals, signage, advertising, etc. All of these are a function of marketing.

1. # of Leads

© 2014

Marketing As a Process

If you're in the "I Hate Marketing Club," I don't blame you. Not one bit. Marketing is only fun for marketers, and most are just guessing at what they do and experimenting with your money. They try something, and when that doesn't work, they'll try something else. It's like gambling—fun and exciting, but you never seem to come away with as much as you spend.

Most business owners see marketing as a necessary evil. But good marketing is measurable and results-driven. And good marketers hold themselves accountable for the *return on investment* (ROI) their clients get from their efforts. Without any marketing, your business isn't likely to grow, or even survive.

The problem is often our perception of what marketing is or what we think it should do. Our definition of marketing is simply:

The *process* of identifying and attracting qualified customers.

Sure, a component of marketing is advertising. It includes research that helps businesses understand who the best buyers are, where they are, what they want, and how to reach them. It has to do with branding and image. But really, all these are just steps in what should be a fluid process that creates new leads, a statistical percentage of which will become buyers.

Since every process is made up of a series of individual distinct steps, what are the steps in an effective marketing process? They begin with careful and thorough market research that aligns products with target customers and tells them that the business has a good fit and a viable product. Then they continue with the steps outlined below.

Why Most Marketing Fails

Most business owners end up being disappointed with their marketing. That's largely because they 'shoot from the hip,' placing ads they like in places that are inexpensive (or free, like social media) instead of thinking from their buyer's perspective and what they will respond to.

We're talking about a lack of strategy—the purpose behind why you are putting your name out there and specifically what you want to get back from any particular ad or campaign. To be clear, the purpose of any and all marketing should be to generate sales. Not leads, not likes, not shares. Sales. If you start thinking in those terms and creating benchmarks by which you measure the success of a campaign, then you can manage your marketing and your marketers for results.

Strategy—Generate More Sales

Countless books have been written on why effective marketing is critical to the success of your business (it is) and how to craft great ads that get the phone ringing. Here, we'll focus on just 3 components of building a marketing strategy that generates sales. This *ABC approach* is a simple process to clarify your purpose and ensure you stay on point.

A—Attract Attention

Like a bee to a flower, you first must get the attention of your target market—the people most interested in your product/service and most likely to buy from you. Ask yourself: What is it that my buyers are looking for right now? Why are they on the market, searching for a new home? What are they most likely to respond to? What can I say or show that will attract their interest and keep their attention so that they'll look closely at my business?

Of those questions, start with the 'why.' Understand that if someone has taken the trouble to find you, either by coming to your sales office or visiting your website, they have a particular and present need—a reason for looking to make a change. Why? Answer that question and address the big 'why' in your headlines and offers, and you'll capture your buyer's attention.

Your attraction message must be relevant to your buying audience. They need to see you, your product/service, and your company as a solution to a particular need; they need to see themselves in the picture you paint with the copy and photography you show them. And that brings us to the 'B' of the ABCs.

B—Benefits

The single biggest mistake that we see from advertising and websites is that they talk about the features of a product or service: bigger, stronger, more efficient, etc. Your buyer doesn't care about the features, he/she cares about what those features can do for them, the benefits.

Instead of bigger, say "it's roomier, more comfortable for your family." Stronger translates into safety: "Your family will be safe, secure, and protected by our above-code construction." Energy efficiency is great, but quantify it: "This home will cost an average of $237 per month less to heat and cool. That's money in your pocket."

The benefits, the "What's in it for me?", is what your buyer is really interested in. The features are just how the benefits are delivered. Talk about your features and your buyers will feel unfulfilled and unimpressed. Show them how those features

29

translate into tangible benefits, and they'll become emotionally involved with your home or community.

C—Call to Action

If you don't ask, you won't get. So, don't be ambiguous in stating what you want your *prospects* to do, the next step or action they should take. If you captured their attention and earned their interest with your benefits, then tell them what to do next.

Amazingly, that's exactly what your buyers *want* you to do. Most of us feel that we hate to be told what to do, but in reality we crave it. When you're on an unfamiliar street, you hope for a road sign (or the voice from your GPS) to tell you where to turn. Your buyers are the same. Buying a new home or moving to a new community is unfamiliar territory for them. When they aren't sure what should happen next, they rely on you to tell them. It's reassuring and helps them muster up the courage to move forward.

So, be clear what you want your prospects to do and why they should do it now:

- "Call now to learn how our new homes can cost you less to own than a used home."
- "Click here to download an area map showing how close you are to everything when you call our community 'home.'"
- "Come in today to experience the comfort and safety of our gated community."
- "Call to schedule a tour of our award-winning model to see how spacious and comfortable your new home will be."

Those are the ABCs of creating an effective marketing strategy. They are all about your buyers and their interests. Use this to create your messaging and graphics, understanding that your prospects get excited when they can see themselves represented in your marketing, and you'll have a good foundation for building marketing campaigns that result in sales.

The Elements of a Lead

Buyers begin as leads—people who express an interest in your product, but are in the early stages of researching your offer. That being the case, how do we attract more leads?

Get Found

For your potential customers or residents to do business with you, they must somehow become aware of your existence; they have to find you. So, the first function of marketing is to appear in your prospect's *search corridor*. That term describes all the places a buyer is likely to look for a solution like yours: Google searches, newspaper, radio, TV, asking their friends on Facebook or Twitter, etc.

Where are homebuyers spending their time searching for their new home? It isn't touring homes and driving from builder to builder, from model to model. Nobody's got time for that! Instead, they are searching for you online.

Current data tells us that 90% of homebuyers will shop your website before they ever come to see you in person.[1] They want to know who you are, if you offer what they are looking for, and if they can trust you enough to pack up the kids, get in the car, and spend a couple of hours of their valuable time talking with you.

Make no mistake. If they can't find you online (i.e., your website or social media presence), they aren't likely to find you at all. Your website, then, is your most important marketing and sales tool.

Getting found will require having an attractive website that is optimized to show up in search engines for key words and phrases that best describe your offering. *Search engine optimization* (SEO) is one of the best investments you can make to ensure you get found by your buyers. SEO strategies might also include a blog and a robust social media presence. The more content you have to share, the more Google, Bing, and Yahoo will be able to rank you higher in their search results.

Words and phrases people use to search for a new home nearly always include a location. So should your website and SEO. "New homes in Springfield, MA" or "builders in Jefferson County, KY" are examples of how people shop. If I'm looking for a home in Raleigh, I'm not going to be interested in a builder from Cleveland, no matter how nice the home. So, make sure you optimize the areas in which you build. An SEO marketing specialist will help you determine the best way to accomplish this for your company and circumstances.

Attention

Once they've found you, you must capture and hold their attention. Given that the average American is subjected to upwards of 250 advertising messages per day (some say the actual figure is closer to *5,000*), that's not an easy task.[2]

Attracting attention requires a bold positioning statement that addresses your viewer's needs and concerns—the discomfort that they're looking to alleviate or solve. And this is where so many companies commit marketing suicide. If you talk about *yourself*—how beautiful your homes are or how long you've been in business—you won't even get noticed. Talk instead about their pain, though, and you'll get their attention. You have to meet them where they are before you can lead them to where they need to be.

Interest

Once you have their attention, you've got to keep it by giving them something interesting to them. And what are your prospects interested in? Themselves! As soon as they see your ad or website, they're asking themselves, "What's here for me? Is this right for my family?" If you can help them see themselves in what you show them (i.e., address their issues or present a question relevant to them), you'll keep their attention.

Your site visitors are looking for something specific. If they don't find it quickly, they're off to the next builder's site. Experts tell us that we have only 3–5 seconds to capture their attention before they click away, even less for a print ad.[3] So it is imperative that your website, literature, and all presentations reflect the things that your target buyers are interested in and looking for.

Too often we see builder's websites and literature that feature nice pictures, but no people. You might put world-class gourmet kitchens in all your houses, but without people they can look like lonely places. So put people in your pictures. Show them enjoying the home. Help your prospects picture themselves in that kitchen, grilling out on the patio, or relaxing with a good book in your atrium. Make the home live in a way that captures your buyer's imagination, and you'll keep their interest.

Buyers are also interested in the opinions and experiences of others. One of the greatest fears that a homebuyer has is that they'll make a mistake, a bad decision. Testimonials from happy homeowners help calm those fears and build trust. All your marketing materials should be peppered with positive comments from past and current customers. Include their pictures; their smiling faces in front of their beautiful homes will grab interest and create the "I want what they've got" feeling. That brings us to the next step.

Desire

Get their interest, and leave them wanting more. Desire for improvement is at the root of every purchase and every buying action. If you can show them an image that makes them say, "That's what I'm talking about," then you're creating desire that will motivate them to take the next step. And if you can back that up with proof that you can deliver, then you're likely to engage that buyer and get them to take you seriously.

When addressing desire, think benefits, not features. Your prospect may really like the tray ceiling you put in the master bedroom, but their real desire might be to move away from their rundown, unsafe neighborhood. In fact, the real motivation behind most home-buying decisions is nearly always to move away from an uncomfortable situation as opposed to moving toward a more positive situation. So, being aware of the core emotions behind motivation and desires is important.

Ask yourself once you find a benefit, what's the benefit of the benefit? In other words, how does it affect them? "Not only do you save $237 per month on energy costs, but imagine what you can do with that money!" Now you are getting to the real buying trigger.

Action

Create the desire, and then tell them what you want them to do to achieve it. Remember, people fear change. It's easier to do nothing than to take action, because action equals change. But create enough desire, and it will outweigh the fear. That's a natural rule in both marketing and sales. Nothing happens without someone taking an action. Clicking a link; submitting a web form; picking up the phone; piling the kids in the car and heading over to your sales office—these are the actions that move the sale forward.

The action you want is for everyone who visits your website or reads your message to jump in their cars, visit your sales center, and buy a home. But most people aren't ready to take that leap the first time they see you. They need to become familiar and comfortable with you, engaging a little at a time. It's much more effective to give them a small step to take first.

A great first step is to offer your web visitors something relevant and of interest to them—a white paper, special report or plan series—that they can download immediately. This requires an action on their part, but a small one. And all they have to do to get the valuable information is give you their name and email address.

For example, a customer builder in North Carolina has created an enticing offer: "Top 5 'Most House for the Money' Home Plans." If you were a potential buyer shopping builders, wouldn't you be interested in plans that offer exceptional value with their use of space? Even if value wasn't your main concern, wouldn't you be compelled to at least see how they achieved that ranking? All you have to do is give your name and email address, and shazzam! The plans appear in your inbox.

Your first transaction has just taken place. Your prospect has taken a small action as a test of your integrity and is rewarded with something that can truly help them make an educated decision to move forward with you. And you now have their contact information so that you can continue to deliver relevant information to them, prompting them to take the next step—to visit you in person.

The Marketing Message

If you've progressed through the steps outlined above, you've seen your *marketing message*, the topic of discussion with your audience, become more clearly defined with every step. It has to be clear, relevant, compelling, and include a strong 'call to action' or incentive to take the next step.

What messages are most compelling? They are always the ones that most closely match the prospect's reasons for considering a purchase. As aforementioned, most people (i.e., 85%) are more motivated to move *away* from a bad situation (pain) than they are to move *toward* a benefit.[4]

Think about it. Which is the more powerful motivation for going to a gym a) to get buff, or b) to avoid having a heart attack? You might be feeling that middle-age spread and know that regular visits to the gym would be of benefit, but unless and

until something changes to create a greater sense of urgency, you're not likely to be motivated to take action.

Likewise, which of the following messages do you think is more compelling?

- "Enjoy the comforts and safety of home in our gated community."
- "Stop wasting money on rent. Own your home today."

You might like the first statement more than the second. It's positive and upbeat and promotes your benefits. It's friendly and safe. Most of us would feel better making that statement than the bolder, more 'in your face' statement about wasting money. The second statement though addresses a pain your audience might already be feeling. In most cases, it would be more motivating than the first one.

Of course, your message should align with your market. The rising cost of renting might be the issue for young couples or first-time buyers. "Stop burning money on sky-high utility bills. Move to the warmth and comfort of an ABC Home!" might resonate with move-up buyers (incorporates both an *away* and a *toward* message). Retirees and active adults may not say it, but as we get older we fear ladders, stairs, and other maintenance risks. How can you frame a message to address those fears and compel buyers to look at your product?

Your marketing message should answer the prospect's issue: "I'm tired of _____." Fill in that blank and provide an answer, and you'll get their attention, interest, desire, and most importantly, action.

Defining Your Message

Your message isn't really your message. It's *their* message, the one your prospects are interested in hearing. Still, the message has to define and differentiate you from all the other builders and communities that your audience will see. This means defining and publishing what is referred to as your *unique selling proposition* (USP).

Your USP tells your prospects what's different about you, while still delivering the "What's in it for me?" message. It gets your audience to say, "Oh, now this is interesting. . ." More clearly defined, your USP is a statement that tells your buyers how you can relate to them in a unique and special way.

To help define and refine you message, answer these 10 questions:

1. Who are my customers?

What are the common traits and characteristics shared by your best or most prevalent buyers? Create demographic and psychographic profiles. What do these reveal about your target market?

2. What do they want?

What is the dominant motive for choosing your home or community? Is it comfort? Safety? Security? Status? You must be able to clearly identify the major physical and emotional needs before you can fill them.

3. What do I want them to do?

Selling is a process that you control. Plan out the process as a series of next steps that you want your buyers to take, the steps that will lead to them realizing what they want and making the purchasing decision. If they're on your website, tell them what to do next, such as register for a special report or call for an appointment. At every juncture in a fluid sales process, there is a logical next step. Make sure you know and communicate what that step is.

4. Why should they choose me?

You know better than your customers what choices they have available to them. So, what makes you their best choice? What can you do or show them that makes you stand out as the one and only home or community for them? There may be two or three benefits that you offer that others don't, or that you do better than anyone else. Make sure those are the things that you feature and communicate continually.

5. What is my Unique Selling Proposition?

In the previous question, you identified what you do better than others. Here, we're looking at your feature/benefit proposal from the customer's viewpoint: What will your customers perceive as unique and special about you? This will become the cornerstone of all your messaging. When you identify and focus on this, you truly begin to become attractive!

6. What is my *customer value proposition* (CVP)?

Your CVP is measured in terms of the customer's return on engagement. What is the payoff for your customers if they engage with you? What is the real value to them? How will your home improve their lives, make them happier or safer, or give them greater peace of mind? Define this and you'll be able to zero in on your prospect's dominant buying motivations—their hot buttons.

7. What is my offer?

Are you ready to make them an offer they can't refuse? If you've accurately answered questions 1–6, then you know this isn't about price. It's about finding the tipping point that helps your customer move from their present pain to your value solution.

8. What is my elevator speech?

This is an important exercise. Describe all the benefits you offer your customers—how your offering improves lives—in 30 seconds or less. Start with this statement: "I help [your specific target buyers] do/realize [your major benefit/USP/CVP] even if [worst case scenario]."

Example: "I help growing families afford comfortable and stylish homes that enhance their lifestyle even when markets are tight and costs are rising."

9. What are my traffic routes?

Where are your buyers shopping? How are they finding you? How do they respond to you when they find you? By phone? Email? Walk-in? Analyzing where your current buyers are coming from will tell you where to focus your marketing.

10. What are my calls to action?

The third question addresses what next step you want your prospects to take. When you've answered that, then you need to tell them what to do next and give them a way to do easily do it. Web forms, 'call us now' campaigns, and timed incentives are all calls to action. If you don't ask, you won't get.

When you've answered all the questions and listened to the candid comments of your buyers, you're ready to begin crafting a message that tells your audience why you are uniquely qualified to offer them the things they most value, and how you've helped others to achieve their dreams.

Tell me a Story

The best marketing messages tell a story that conveys your benefits so your prospects can understand and relate to it And the best marketing strategies employ and often revolve around a story line.

For example, pay attention to the next Subaru commercial you see on TV. The car maker doesn't brag about their safety features or how long their vehicles last. Instead, they illustrate their key benefits through customer stories: a man whose Subaru has been his faithful companion through the years; a woman whose daughter has grown up in the back seat of her car. Both of these story lines convey not just the safety and security of the car, but also the emotional benefits that come with it.

What's your story? Likely, you'll find it crafted through customer testimonials combined with your own rich history of satisfying buyers and caring for families. Work on your story first and the delivery vehicle second.

If you follow these tips, you'll create a powerful message that will attract the people you want as customers—those whose values are aligned with yours.

Delivering the Message: Marketing Vehicles

Marketing has two functions: Creating leads, as we've been discussing, and then nurturing those leads, that is, building on their interest once they've taken an initial action. There are several tools to help your business accomplish these functions:

Website

Your website should be visually compelling so that it instantly captivates your viewer's interest. A stunning image on a light background (white is best) gets and keeps attention. Add a strong opening USP statement that addresses your audience's interests, needs, and values.

Make sure your site is easy to navigate, with buttons clearly labeled showing visitors how to find your plans, photos, and an idea of your price ranges. As mentioned earlier, at least some of your photos should be of people—similar to your demographic audience—enjoying themselves in your home.

And it is essential that you include a lead magnet and strong call to action. A downloadable "Top 5 'Most House For The Money' Home Plans" might be offered if you're a value builder. When prospects click the 'get it' button, they fill out a brief form with their name and email address. If you sell to different buyer groups, you could ask them to choose which series they were most interested in: starter homes, move-up homes, or empty-nester homes. Deliver the requested plan via email, and launch an automated follow-up campaign to nurture interest.

Finally, your site should use SEO so that your buyers find you when they search relevant words or phrases. This should be set up and monitored by a professional service provider. If you want good results, then "don't try this at home!"

Paid Media

Print media, such as newspapers and real estate magazines, can still be effective and should remain a part of your marketing mix. But more effective are online advertising opportunities. Paid search (*pay-per-click* or PPC) advertising allows you to reach a very targeted audience, and you only pay for leads that take an action that indicates strong interest. That makes such campaigns highly cost effective and allows you to test different messages against a baseline for continued improvement.

Events

Home shows, Tour of Homes, local fairs, etc., anywhere you can be face to face with your community can still be effective *marketing vehicles*. They are highly visual and keep you in the public eye, so they are wonderful publicity. But you can probably come up with other opportunities to bring buyers onto your sales floor and into your model. Consider these events:

- Host a Chamber of Commerce After Hours meeting in your model.
- Register your sales center as a Toys for Tots or food drive drop-off point.
- Sponsor a fund raiser for a local charity.
- Host a showing for a local artist.

Given that events are great publicity and often get media coverage, what other opportunities can you think of to get more people into your model to experience your home in person?

Social Media—Think *Conversations*

Social media is all about sharing. When people share your message, it is, in effect, a third-party endorsement of you and your product. People trust recommendations and endorsements from their friends. So, an active social media program is highly recommended.

The old way to advertise was to run an ad to promote an open house or sale. But those ads get tuned out today. We know that we don't begin to get buyer's attention until they've seen us 3–5 times, and that even in a direct sales situation 80% of sales take place after the 5th contact.[5] So, think in terms of conversations instead of statements.

That's where social media excels, and why businesses of every sort are moving marketing funds from traditional advertising to training personnel to maintain active Facebook pages, Twitter streams, and blogs (or outsourcing their social media management altogether.) The objective is to engage prospects in conversations, to tell your story and to let your buyers tell theirs. Do this while building your brand and letting your happy customers brag about you.

A word of caution: Don't start unless you are committed to keeping it up. A Facebook page with no recent activity is worse than no page at all. When people don't see new posts regularly (at least 3–5 times per week), they tend to think something is wrong. That's not the message you want to publish.

That said, Facebook and Pinterest are perfect places to share photos and testimonials. YouTube is the second most-frequented search engine on the planet, so posting video walkthroughs of your homes and communities should be considered mandatory. Twitter is a wonderful medium to promote open houses and events. And Google+ gets strong search-engine coverage because, well . . . it's Google!

How are you engaging your prospects and your residents in interesting and relevant conversations? That's word-of-mouth advertising at its best!

Public Relations

Local news broadcasts and papers need one vital element to attract views and subscribers: news. So, make sure they can find it at your sales center or community. Current in-demand topics that make headlines include energy efficiency, cutting-edge design, green construction methods, and affordable housing. Press releases that address these or similar topics can get a reporter or news crew to your site and introduce your product to thousands of potential buyers at no charge to you.

Controversy also attracts news. Are financing or permitting laws changing or being challenged in your area? Offer your commentary as a local expert on the topic, or write an article or response to articles already published.

Realtor Program

Unless you're brand new to the industry, you probably have opinions regarding Realtors. Perhaps you've tried to get real estate agents to refer prospects to you in the past, but without success. Or maybe you've come to the conclusion that realtors are just down right lazy and not worth the time or effort to cultivate.

You might be right, of course. Your opinions are most likely born from experience, and we're not going to argue with you. Many Realtors are just as described above. But not all.

The success of an effective Realtor Program is just like that of any marketing initiative: you're looking for the right people, who understand the value of what you have to offer. As with buyers, that takes some education. If more Realtors understood the value of the investment your home or community represents, they'd be delighted to make a referral. Most don't; but some do. Focus on attracting a) those who appreciate what you have, and b) those who specialize in working with the type of customers you want.

Of course, Realtors work for a fee, usually around 3% of the sale price (you can negotiate on rentals, too). So, why would they work with you rather than selling an existing home for more money? Simple: they can only sell what the buyer can afford to buy. You're the affordable-housing expert, remember? You've got an alternative to what might otherwise be no *commission* at all.

Here are some ways to attract the right Realtors:

- Include your sales center on a Tour of Homes. Every real estate office has one each week.
- Realtor Lunch—Yes, agents will show up for a free lunch, and they just might learn something.
- Office presentations—Ask to speak at their weekly sales meeting and present your product.

Networking

You've probably heard the saying, "It's not what you know, it's who you know." It's trite, but true. Great salespeople are master networkers. They cultivate relationships with anyone and everyone who can help them find more buyers and sell more homes. They are tireless self-promoters. And it pays off.

First, who do you know? We've already mentioned your contacts at the Chamber of Commerce, but what about other local associations? The Rotary Club, Kiwanis, Knights of Columbus, Home Builders Association, etc. are all places you can connect with influencers in a position to refer and recommend you to others they know. And referral sales are the easiest and most lucrative leads you'll ever find.

Each of these associations and many more like them have regular meetings and are always looking for new speakers. Put together a presentation about the benefits and value of your product, polish it, and take your show on the road.

Signage

It's old school, I know, but signage is an important part of your image and your marketing promotions. Keep your sales center signs clearly visible and fresh at all times. Keep your site signs well lit at night, and make sure landscaping doesn't hide them.

And don't forget lot signs. Posting a plan of the ideal model that would fit a specific lot on the lot sign is a great way to help the less imaginative picture what their home might look like when finished on that lot.

Referrals

This one is so big that it has its own chapter. See Chapter 4 page 63.

Lead Nurture/Follow-Up Tools

The very best follow-up is always in person. Nothing is more personal or effective. But, of course, that isn't always practical. To not follow up is to ignore your prospect, and if you ignore them, you will almost certainly lose them. So employing effective ways to deliver your message is critical. We recommend a mix of the following tools.

Phone

The second-best method is by phone. It's personal; the listener can hear your voice and inflection, and it tells your prospect that he is worth your time and effort. And therein lies the rub—it requires your time and effort. So most salespeople don't call nearly as much as they should. Don't let that be you.

Excuses for not calling are that you don't have anything new to say, or that the prospect probably won't be home anyway, so why call? But those excuses simply don't hold water.

First, if you can't think of something new to share with your prospect that would warrant a phone call, then you're just not putting any effort into it. A new plan, a new feature that is being introduced, a local news item that affects local housing, a reduced inventory due to increased sales activity, time running out on a promotion—all these can be reasons to prompt a phone conversation that shows your prospect that you're thinking of them.

What if they're not at home? Leave a voice mail! Yes, your message will be heard. I recommend that salespeople always have a script about 30–45 seconds long ready. An example might be:

> Hi, Jim. This is Scott with ABC Builders. I'm calling to personally thank you for your interest in our beautiful line of energy efficient homes. Did you know that a new ABC Home could cut your utilities bills in half? Why not stop by our model at 345 Summit St. in Springfield to learn more and see why there's never been a better time to build a new home! You can call me at 456-555-1212. Again, this is Scott with ABC Builders at 456-555-1212, and I look forward to speaking with you soon. Thanks.

That example is personal, asks a question that piques the prospect's interest ("Did you know . . ."), and offers a kind but specific call to action ("Why not stop by . . ."). Yes, you can accomplish *a lot* by phone and voicemail if you put some effort into it.

Email

Even though it is perceived as impersonal, email is probably the primary nurture method available to you, particularly if you're employing the lead-magnet strategy outlined earlier. Emails are the most requested means of communication, so use them to their fullest by scheduling regular emails with pertinent information relevant to individual buyer's interest. (See Chapter 3 for details.)

Direct Mail

There was a time about eight years ago when direct mail had lost much of its effectiveness. Junk mail was at a high, and most direct mail pieces never made it past the circular file. Not so today. The cost of mailing has risen, so junk mail has switched to email (just check your spam folder). So your direct mail promotions are much more likely to be opened and read.

Photo postcards with compelling photography of a home is a prime example. These are still the featured posts of thousands of American refrigerators. So use them, and always include a call to action.

Social Media

We've already discussed social media as a lead-creation tool, but it's equally useful as a follow-up tool. When someone posts a comment on a post, always follow up with a kind response thanking the commenter for his or her input. Use your blog and social forums to answer FAQs or to feature stories about your homeowners and their experiences. Social media is the Swiss Army knife of marketing; you'll continue to find new ways to use it and share your marketing message.

Getting the Most From the Leads You Have Through Marketing Automation

Marketing is a means to an end—sales. If you intend to find new business, you're going to have to face the fact that you'll need to engage in some type of marketing and promotions, be it a print ad, your website, or just word of mouth. Bottom line: No marketing, no sales. No sales, no money.

Will more marketing result in more sales? Is increasing your marketing budget the best way to increase sales, revenues, and profits? Yes and no. Increasing your marketing will bring in more leads and prospects. But is that the *best* way to increase sales? Not necessarily. It could be that you can make more sales from the leads you already have or are generating.

Increasing Marketing Return on Investment

It is often difficult to measure the effectiveness of a single ad or marketing campaign. And that's really the key, isn't it? To establish your return on investment from your marketing spend? It should be easy: Marketing costs divided by number of leads = cost per lead. Marketing costs divided by number of sales = cost per sale.

We're continually shocked and dismayed at the number of business owners who don't stop to calculate these costs. You can't manage what you don't measure. What you do measure is likely to improve. Marketing is just too expensive a line item not to measure and monitor carefully.

Once you begin measuring it, how do you increase your *marketing ROI*? You can create better ads that generate more leads. Or, you can do a better job with the leads you're already getting. That's the first area we address with our clients—make sure our nurturing and sales processes are polished before we throw more money at advertising.

Start With Your Processes

What happens when you get a new lead? Who gets the lead, what do they do with it, and how long does it take before action is taken?

Here's what probably happens: A lead comes in as a response from your website or online presence (my builder clients tell me that over 80% of their leads come from this source), and someone in your office is notified that there is a new lead. They send an email to a sales rep that there is an "inquiry from the website" that they need to follow up on. Several hours (days?) later, the salesperson checks his email and sees the new lead and immediately thinks, "Oh, brother. Another tire kicker. These Internet leads never pan out." A couple of days go by before the inquiry gets a response, and by that time, they've already moved on to one or more of your competitors.

Don't believe me? I hope you're right, that your business is one of the 3% of small businesses that have an effective follow-up system.[6] But unless you're measuring and monitoring these activities, you really don't know, do you?

Now, what *should* happen? As figure 2.1 shows, a lead comes in from your website, and it includes name and contact information, along with what product or service the person is interested in. Immediately, an automated email is sent thanking them for their interest, delivering some answers or information that is specifically relevant to their stated interest, and promising them that a representative will be in contact with them shortly. An invitation is also included for them to call or visit your office or model.

FIGURE 2.1 Automated system flowchart

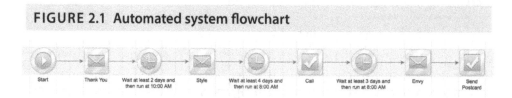

An automated system immediately assigns the lead to a sales rep and schedules a time to respond to the new lead. A task is placed on their calendar and notes are included as to the prospect's interests.

Prior to the scheduled call, a pop-up reminder appears on the sales rep's calendar and an email is sent to him (and a copy to the sales manager) that he has an assigned task or call to make.

The call is made, and notes are added to the contact file as to what was discussed. Or, a message is left on their voicemail. In that case, a "Sorry I missed you" email is automatically sent (pre-written; the sales rep just pushes a button).

An automated campaign consisting of emails, phone calls, and/or messages, postcards, or letters is implemented, building on the prospect's stated interests, giving them more benefits that you can offer and encouraging them to call for an appointment or jump in their cars to come see you.

Why You Need to Polish Your Processes

You can either a) do no marketing and wait for business to come to you (i.e., the 'hope' strategy); b) throw more money into more ad campaigns that bring in more leads, most of which won't be properly worked; or c) install processes that make sure every lead gets the full attention it deserves and is nurtured and cultivated effectively. This will mean more sales from existing leads, lowering your cost per lead and cost per sale, and increasing your marketing ROI, your sales, and your profits.

Here are some statistics you should consider:

- 90% or more of your leads are shopping and learning about you online.[7]
- 97% of your website visitors leave your site without ever telling you who they are.[8]
- Online inquiries expect a response within seconds. Wait just 2 hours and you've lost 90% of them.[9]
- Follow-up is still the name of the game. 80% of all sales are made between the 5th and 12th contact; most salespeople give up after 3 contact attempts.[10]

Installing systems and processes to better address the needs and interests of your prospects and nurture their interest in your product is by far the most cost effective route you can take. Such systems are affordable and customized for your specific business and needs; they free up your sales staff to spend their time on the more qualified leads and actually work to generate more sales from fewer leads.

Most importantly, they make your entire business work better and generate more cash flow and profits. Isn't it time you implemented marketing and sales automation into your business?

Marketing 'By the Numbers'

Here's where the real science comes in: You must constantly and consistently employ processes that accurately monitor and measure your marketing effectiveness. That requires the right tools and a strategy to put them to use.

Lead Generation

Why are we marketing again? Oh yeah . . . we need more sales, and sales come from leads, which come from marketing. Yes, but how much is enough? Begin by answering these questions:

- How many leads do I need to meet sales quota?
- Where are my best sales or residents coming from?
- What is my average cost per lead? Cost per sale?
- What if . . .
  - » I increase marketing expenditure by 10%?
  - » I decrease marketing expenditure by 10%?
  - » I increase visitor-to-lead conversion by 100%? 200%? 300%?

Start with the first question. How many leads do you need to achieve your sales goals? You answer that question with a simple equation:

Target sales goal _____ ÷ conversion rate _____ = Number of leads _____

If your goal is to sell 50 homes per year, and you sell one home for every 20 presentations you make (5% conversion rate), then the formula is:

Target sales goal 50 ÷ conversion rate 0.05 = Number of leads 1,000

You'll need to make 1,000 presentations to sell 50 homes. That's about 4 presentations per day, 5 days per week, for 50 weeks out of the year. But we're discussing marketing here, not sales. So the real question is: *How many people must you reach in order to generate 1,000 presentations?*

A typical website only gets a conversion of about 3% of the site visitors that will fill out a contact form or call you.[11] Of those, 10% might turn into presentations. So to generate 1,000 presentations, you'll need 10,000 contact forms, and to do that, you'll need to generate approximately 350,000 unique visitors per year to your website—nearly 1,000 site visitors per day.

When you begin to do that math, the numbers can be frightening. Maybe that's why so few of us keep track of these statistics. But sticking your head in the sand and refusing to do the math just means that either you won't get the leads you need to reach your goals, or you'll probably spend too much on marketing and advertising.

Marketing 'by the numbers,' that is, measuring and tracking these statistics in your company, is the only way to control your marketing costs and effectiveness and ensure you reach your sales goals. The good news is that, once you begin monitoring, you'll find ways to increase your effectiveness and reduce costs.

Create "By The Numbers" Marketing Goals and Strategies

First, determine what you need. In Chapter 1, you learned how to start with the end in mind. Remember how Art Vandelay turned his business around? He started by setting a profit goal:

- To achieve $30,000 in profit required $500,000 in revenue.
- To achieve $500,000 in revenue required 1,000 sales at $500 per sale.
- To get 1,000 sales, at a closing rate of $25%, he needed to generate 800 leads.

Are you generating the number of leads you need to reach your sales goals? If not, using the simple formula that Art used, determine how many more leads you'll need and what you'll need to do to get them.

Be specific, and write out the marketing goal using this format:

_____ _____ from _____ to _____ by _____.
   (Verb)   (Noun)   (Number) (Number)   (Date)

The verb is usually increase, decrease, or maintain. Then, in order to meet this goal, state what strategy you'll employ:

_____ _____ by _____, _____, & _____.
   (Verb)   (Noun) by   (Action)   (Action) and (Action)

After reviewing the effectiveness of all available advertising methods, determine which ones you'll focus on to achieve your lead goal. As an example, your goal-setting statement might be:

Increase qualified leads from 17 to 24 by June 2015.

Your strategy might be:

Increase leads by increasing paid search by 50%, employing a strong SEO program, and launching a nurture program for new Internet leads.

Once you've identified strategies (the "how you are going to achieve your goal"), it is time to create action plans. Action plans are a numbered list of required tasks. Each task has four components: task name, responsible party, due date, and completion status (table 2.1).

TABLE 2.1 Marketing strategy implementation

Task	Assigned to	Due Date	Completed
Research key words	John	April 1	March 28
Select Search Engines	Pat	April 5	
Define PPC budget	John, Barb	April 5	April 3
Contact SEO company	John	April 12	
Write nurture campaign	Sandy	April 12	

Once you've completed your action plan, you should evaluate the strategy's costs, effectiveness, and return on investment.

3

Sales Conversion Rate (#2 of 7)

The sole purpose of your marketing is to bring in qualified buyers. Your proficiency in converting leads to sales is the second of the 7 Key Numbers that you should be keenly interested in on a daily basis.

Is selling a process? Absolutely! But how that process is employed must be adapted to each individual buyer, and that's something a lot of salespeople struggle with.

The thing to remember is that selling a new home might be your job, but it's your buyer's *journey*. The path they take, the speed with which they move, and the things that are important along the way are all up to them. Whether you fulfill your job and make the sale depends on how well you align *your processes* with *their journey*.

Joining Buyers on Their Journey

Salespeople need to get a better handle on how people buy and match the sales process to your prospect's buying process. After all, that's what drives the purchasing decision.

A lot of salespeople still talk *at* prospects instead of to or with them. They spew features of their homes without really considering whether or not they're what their prospect wants, needs, or is willing to listen to. Instead, lay the sales process down on one side, then put yourself on the other side with the buyer and ask, "What are they doing? What's their process?" Then, arrange your process to align with theirs.

TABLE 3.1 Buying stage—seller role

Buying Stage	Seller Role
Change	Student
Discontent	Doctor
Research	Architect
Comparison	Coach
Fear	Therapist
Commitment	Negotiator
Expectation	Teacher
Satisfaction	Farmer

Source: *Getting Into Your Customer's Head: 8 Secret Roles of Selling Your Competitors Don't Know* by Kevin Davis (New York: Crown Publishing Group, 1996).

In his classic book, *Getting Into Your Customer's Head: 8 Secret Roles of Selling Your Competitors Don't Know*, Kevin Davis turns the old critical path sales approach on its ear and instead offers eight specific buying stages that prospects go through (and how decisions are made at each stage). He then outlines eight corresponding roles that salespeople must embrace to help them align their thinking with their buyer's thinking at each stage (table 3.1).

For example, your sales process might typically begin with meet and greet. But that's not always the first thing on your prospect's list. They may be concerned with other questions that need to be addressed before they can relax and get to know you. So, you need to be aware and adaptable so you can follow the customer's lead and keep them engaged.

I once had an appointment with a family that, on the phone, sounded desperate for a new home. I was watching for them as they pulled into the sales center. Now, our entrance was beautifully landscaped, and the model was set to show off its best features. In other words, we were optimized for the WOW effect. But none of that mattered to this couple.

As they approached the door, I was waiting with a big smile on my face and hand extended in greeting. She blew right past me, walked right to our table, sat down, and looked me straight in the eye. "You said on the phone you could build large custom kitchens. Well, let's talk about my kitchen," was all she said.

This prospect wasn't interested in a meet and greet, in me, or small talk. She was there on a mission. I obliged by immediately grabbing my pad and pencil as she described an outrageously large kitchen, one that would be better suited in a 5-star restaurant than in a home. I listened carefully for a few minutes, dutifully taking notes, before asking, "You realize this is an exceptionally large amount of space you're requesting. Do you mind if I ask why you need such a large kitchen?" In the next few minutes, I learned volumes.

Two weeks prior, her entire family had come to her small home for Thanksgiving dinner. She, her sister, and their mother were all trying to occupy the same space at the same time as they each prepared their part of the meal . . . and it was a huge disaster. Determined never to experience that again, she determined that she needed a big kitchen.

Armed with a clear understanding of what the real need was, I was able to properly demonstrate the kitchen in my model home now that I knew the real motivation for her being on the market and in my sales center. So, this illustrated both why you need to be sensitive to where your buyer wants to start the process, as well as why you should always look for ways to ask the 'why' question.

The "Happening"

Every buyer is on the market for a specific reason, and each buyer's reason differs from the next. Kerry Mulcrone, author of *Model Home, Model Store*, suggests we look for the "happening"—the specific change in circumstances that has created the need for a new home. "It could already have happened, or it could be about to happen, but everyone has a happening that puts them on the market. Your goal as a salesperson is to discover and clearly understand that happening," offers Mulcrone. "Do that, and you'll understand their motivation and be able to keep their sense of urgency high."

When you can identify that "happening" early in the process, then you can keep in sync with them. If you fail to get in sync with your buyers, then you'll never be able to fully convey your worth and value to them. If you're trying to gather information in the discovery phase while they're trying to understand what they can get within their budget, then you aren't moving together and there's no basis for agreement. In that case, both processes, the buying *and* the selling, stall out.

Finding Alignment and Agreement

The key is to ask questions that lead to conversations, because it's only through conversation that you'll come to fully understand what Mulcrone calls the "is/did/will happening." When asking open-ended questions, be sure to explain that the reason you're asking is so that you can best help them to achieve their objective; that you're just there to serve them.

For example: "I'm so excited to see you out today, and there's so much here to see. Please, though, share with me what brings you out today so that I'll know what to show you and how best to help you. At the end of this visit, what I want to do is what you need me to do."

Serious buyers, the ones that you want to spend your time with, are craving for someone to understand their needs and help them. But it has to be in a way that they can grasp and feel comfortable with. "We can never throw out the sales process," says Mulcrone, "but we have to make sure it gels with our buyers." In other words, know the steps that need to be taken to move the sales along, but the customer will dictate the order in which you'll take them.

Why Salespeople Fail

New and untrained salespeople often lack the confidence and patience to understand that it's the customer's journey, not their own. Sales coach, Jeff Shore, calls this your "comfort addiction." You're uncomfortable talking about your buyer's problem and feel the need to control the process instead of giving your buyers the opportunity to unfold it for you. "We don't need to be 'large and in charge,'" explains Kerry Mulcrone. That might be the number one killer of sales today. Instead, ask the bold questions—the ones that uncover the real needs; be a keen listener and let the customer take the lead when appropriate. You know the steps that need to be covered and can make sure that they are all addressed in time.

If you try to push your process at your customer and make them conform to your plan, then you'll likely lose them quickly. On the other hand, if at the end of the visit you've helped your buyer accomplish what they came in to do or achieve, then you've moved the sale forward.

Increasing Conversion Rate

Wouldn't it be great if every lead became a prospect, then a customer? Sadly, that doesn't happen. You can't win them all. But you *can* improve your conversion rate and win more sales.

What do we mean by conversion rate? Simply put, the percentage of leads that become customers or residents.

We're really going to talk about four separate conversions:

1. The number of people aware of you that become *leads*—that raise their hand and show some interest.
2. The number of leads that become *prospects*—serious in-the-door interest.
3. The number of those prospects that become *buyers*—your customers.
4. Customers to evangelists—referrals.

© 2014

Awareness to Interest

Fact: 97% of people that visit your website (if it's a good website) leave without letting you know who they are or giving you the chance to market to them.[12] They've moved on and left you no forwarding address.

So, let's assume the following:

Visitors	Lead Rate	Prospect Rate	Sales Conversion Rate
5,000	3% (150)	20% (30)	10% (3)

Marketing is going to focus on delivering more site visitors through increased search engine optimization, pay-per-click, or additional media advertising. Sales are going to focus on better sales training and techniques to increase the sales conversion rate. Both mean your spending additional funds.

However, if you focus on raising the middle two numbers—converting more site visitors into leads and nurturing those leads to take positive action—you can increase the number of prospects that go to the sales team without increasing your marketing spend.

Visitors	Lead Rate	Prospect Rate	Sales Conversion Rate
5,000	3% (150)	20% (30)	10% (3)
5,000	5% (250)	20% (50)	10% (5)
5,000	9% (450)	20% (90)	10% (9)

Converting Visitors to Leads

How do you get more website visitors to give you their name and contact information? By giving them something they want or will find valuable in trade. Lead magnets are what marketing consultant Jerry Rouleau used to call ethical bribes, enticements that turn invisible browsers into identifiable leads that you can continue to reach with your sales message.

Have you ever been in a grocery store and been offered a free sample of a product? Why do they do that? First, it catches your attention. Second, it establishes interest. And third, if you take a taste, then chances are you'll want more. Sales of these products soar when free samples are offered.

Your lead magnets need to work the same way to attract attention, pique interest, and motivate a small response and a desire for more. So, what is it that your site visitors are thinking about or searching for when they click onto your website? Give them a taste in exchange for their contact information.

For example, if you sell starter homes to first-time buyers, you may offer a free report: *10 Essential Facts You Must Know Before Buying Your First Home*. If you are marketing a community, you could offer an area guide showing the major shopping, schools, hospitals, and traffic routes surrounding your community. In both cases, in order to receive the offer, a person must complete a brief form and supply you with their name, email address, and perhaps a phone number, as shown in figure 3.1.

FIGURE 3.1 Converting website visitors to leads with a lead magnet

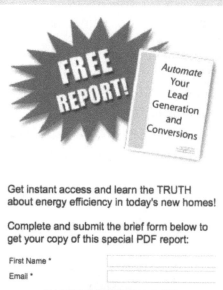

Get instant access and learn the TRUTH about energy efficiency in today's new homes!

Complete and submit the brief form below to get your copy of this special PDF report:

First Name *

Email *

Send me the report!

Now, you have an engaged lead—someone who has taken an action to indicate interest in what you have. You also have a name and email address so you can follow up with them.

Nurturing Leads to Prospects

From your lead magnet, you learned two important things: 1) what the person who submitted your form was interested in; 2) who they are and how to reach them. Now, simply build on their interest by delivering consistent messages that address their stated interest and reinforce your company as the solution they're looking for through a nurture campaign.

According to a DemandGen Report, on average, nurtured leads produce a 20% increase in sales opportunities versus nonnurtured leads.[13] Nurture campaigns should involve as many methods of interaction as possible—email, direct mail, and phone calls—and should be focused on escalating the person's interest to the next step, usually an in-person appointment. The reality is that in most cases you're probably only going to have an email address, at least at first. That's okay; emails can include powerful visuals and calls to action and are still the best means of communication with leads and prospects.

Here's where your strategy needs to be clearly defined. Establish exactly what you want the readers to do next and give them multiple reasons *based on their interests* to take that action. This should be done as a series of emails, each one offering one new compelling fact, links to your website or landing page, and a call to action to contact you.

"But what if I don't get any response?" you might ask. Simple. Do it again. You already know that the person filled out the form on your site because they had an interest; they were ready to take at least some action, so don't give up. They may just need a little more heat applied to get them hot enough to pick up the phone and call you or come into your office. And don't be afraid of offending them by continuing to reach out to them. If they're no longer interested, they'll opt out of your emails. But if you don't reach out to them, you'll never get the response you want. Figure 3.2 shows a typical map of a nurture campaign.

The campaign begins when the prospect submits a form from your website, usually requesting something specific and relevant to them, such a special report or a group of plans that you've singled out. That is followed by a series of automated communications designed to build on the prospect's interest and get him motivated enough to take the next action—to call or visit you in person. Those communications can be emails, letters, postcards, and/or phone calls automatically scheduled for the assigned salesperson.

FIGURE 3.2 Map of a typical nurture campaign

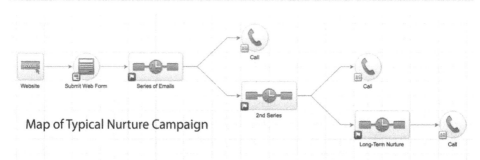

Map of Typical Nurture Campaign

Notice that each sequence of communication ends with either the prospect taking action or another campaign, more communication. Keep reaching out to them through predefined, automated campaigns until they act or tell you they are no longer interested. We know that buyers act on their own schedule. You may be reaching out to people that have a strong interest in your product, but simply aren't in a position to move forward . . . yet. A nurture program allows you to remain in the minds of these future buyers so that when they are ready, you're the first company they call.

If you use a marketing automation/client relationship management system to monitor this, then all sequences stop the moment the prospect takes action. And once you have an in-person contact, that's when the selling begins.

So by focusing on the individual steps of the process, without increasing the amount of advertising spend or our overall market exposure, we're delivering up to 3 times more prospects into the sales funnel. Our numbers now look like this:

Visitors	Lead Rate	Prospect Rate	Sales Conversion Rate
5,000	9% (450)	30% (135)	10% (13.5)

Compare that with our original numbers (3 sales from 5,000 site visitors) that started this discussion. Do you think investing a meager amount of time and implementing marketing automation tools to get a 600% – 900% increase in delivered sales is reasonable? Us too.

Converting Prospects into Sales

So far, your lead magnets and nurture campaigns have accomplished two things:

© 2014

- More leads have been captured from the website;
- More of those leads have entered the sales pipeline as prospects.

But a third function has also taken place. The prospects that are now sitting down with you and your sales team are more informed, better qualified, and require less work to close. Why?

Over the course of your nurture campaign, you've established your interest in doing business with them. You've allowed them to get to know you and given them multiple reasons to trust you. If they didn't like you by now, they wouldn't be in your sales office or on the phone with you. So, the first job of a salesperson—establishing rapport and trust—has already been largely accomplished. The remaining steps are reinforcement of the message, selection, and transaction.

Easier doesn't mean that it's done for you. Selling skills are still required, and you and your product must still live up to the expectations set in the nurture message. But, in general, those prospects that respond to those messages are closer to making the buying decision than those who haven't had that opportunity to get to know you.

And that brings up one more point about your nurture message. It is the first part of your sales message, and it creates a natural bridge or flow from marketing into sales. That being said, it's important that both your marketing and sales teams be involved in crafting the messages that are included in your nurture campaigns, using only the most compelling selling points while still setting realistic expectations.

Managing the Sales Process

You can't manage what you don't measure. Savvy sales managers know that you don't manage salespeople; you manage actions by measuring results.

Here again is where a good *customer relationship management* (CRM) system is essential to measuring, documenting, reporting, and managing sales results. By monitoring the number of leads coming into the sales pipeline and through each step of the sales process, you can manage for predictable results, no matter the market. You'll be able to forecast revenues and plan for expenditures realistically and instantly. It's all about watching the numbers. As an example, consider the sales pipeline shown in figure 3.3:

This figure simply shows the number of people in each step of the sales process. And by the way, whether you've clearly defined it or not, you do have a sales process—the steps and actions that you and your team take with every home you sell and build. If you haven't outlined that process on paper, then I urge you to do so now. Again, the principle is that you can't manage what you don't measure. Defining each step, the actions involved, and who is responsible for those actions can save you untold hours of wasted time and help you streamline and continually refine those processes.

The figure shows 19 new leads during this period, 14 leads in our nurture stage being given additional reasons to take the plunge and schedule an appointment, another 14 that have scheduled a model tour, and so on. Take some time to study the figure. There are a lot of steps included as part of the sales process. Perhaps your funnel doesn't have that many steps. Or maybe you see some steps that you should be including. You may even have some stages in your pipeline that aren't included in the illustration.

FIGURE 3.3 Sales pipeline

Sales Pipeline	
New Lead	19
Nurture 1	14
Prospect	11
Model Tour	14
New Opportunity	9
Proposal	5
Purchase	5
Plans Completed, Stamped	1
Delivery Scheduled	2
Foundation verified	0
Delivered	5
Punch List Complete	4
Testimonial Requested	4
Testimonial Received	12
Loyalty Program	14
Settings	

In any case, considering theses stages and how they apply to your business is important. It highlights the fact that each step is an opportunity to measure, and then to manage that part of the process while increasing efficiency and pull-through.

At each stage of the processes, your question should be, "What is the average number of people that progress from the last stage into this stage? How can I increase that average?"

Of the nine people identified as new opportunities, for example, you should be keenly aware of how well your sales presentations and discovery processes are converting those buyers to the next stage, a proposal. When you can see these numbers clearly, you can measure the effectiveness of your marketing, sales training, and management processes. You can identify areas where improvement is needed and address these quickly. These are vital numbers that every business owner should have instant access to and be engrossed with to determine where you spend your time and money. By improving these numbers, you improve the health of your business.

If you're trying to keep up with these constantly changing numbers by hand or on a spreadsheet, well, how's that working for you? Even when you can see the value of knowing and monitoring each of these numbers, the time required to keep up with them by hand is simply overwhelming. It is not likely to happen.

Instead, an automated customer relationship management system will display these numbers—and others like them—instantly and in real time, giving you a clear picture of your business at just a glance. That's why you need a CRM system to manage your business; it shows you which areas need managing and compares your actual numbers to your expected goals at each step of the process.

Once you get accustomed to managing the process, managing the activities that produce optimum results becomes so much easier. Bottom line, what if you could increase your sales effectiveness by 30% just by managing and streamlining each step of the process? Compare the chart below to the previous one(s):

Visitors	Lead Rate	Prospect Rate	Sales Conversion Rate
5,000	9% (450)	30% (135)	20% (27)

By increasing the sales conversion from 10% of prospects to 20% of prospects in the funnel (and remember, the average increase from a nurture program is 300%), you've captured another 13 sales from the same marketing and the same number of leads. That's what marketing and sales automation can do for you and your sales, and why we feel so strongly that you should be using a marketing automation system.

Setting Conversion Strategies

First, determine what you need. In the example we've been using, we've increased the number of leads that become opportunities from 20% to 30% and the number of converted sales from 10% to 20%. Our goal statement might read:

Increase conversion rate from 10% to 15% by June 2015.

Our strategy statement might be:

Increase our conversion rate by improving objection handling techniques, improving closing techniques, and building a follow-up system.

Use this following formula to state your new sales goals:

_____ _____ from _____ to _____ by _____.

    (Verb)   (Noun)   (Number) (Number)   (Date)

In order to meet this goal, we will:

_____ _____ by _____, _____, & _____.

  (Verb)   (Noun)   by   (Action)   (Action) and   (Action)

Once you've identified strategies (the "how you are going to achieve your goal"), it is time to create action plans. Action plans are a numbered list of required tasks. Each task has four components: task name, responsible party, due date, and completion status.

Once you've completed your action plan, you should evaluate the strategy's costs, effectiveness, and return on investment. But we're not finished yet. Read on to see how CRM helps you manage the rest of your most vital numbers.

4 Generating Upsells, Resells, and Referrals (#3 & #4 of 7)

The easiest sales are to people you've already sold to and to the people they refer to you. The third of the 7 Key Numbers measures how well we increase sales with add-ons and upsells, and the fourth measures what might be the most important metric of all, referrals sales. Do you have a formalized program to reach out to your past and existing customers? If not, this chapter will be invaluable to you!

#3 of 7: Customer Retention

What kind of experience are you creating for your customers? How do they feel after they purchase? Why should you care? The two experiences shared below, one is mine and the other a friend of mine, answer that question:

3. Customer Retention

Upsells & Referrals

© 2014

It's not that I'm pessimistic, but I rarely expect an exceptional experience as a customer.

I travel a fair amount, mostly in the service of clients who hire me to speak at their company or group meetings or to consult on their sales or marketing processes. In order to be as frugal as possible with my client's expense account, I usually shop out airline tickets, rental cars, and motels online and choose the best deals available.

My experience has been that most of these service providers are basically the same. I've come to expect that I'll get to the rental car agency, wait in line while an impersonal agent shuffles through waiting customers until it's my turn, then endure the hard sell as they try to get me to buy their extras—insurance, pre-paid fuel, etc. That's true of just about all of the name brand rental shops.

However, on a recent trip to Chicago, I had a different experience. My best deal from Hotwire.com brought me to Enterprise Rent-A-Car for the first time in a long while. Here's what happened:

I stepped off of the shuttle to be greeted by a well-dressed young man who opened the door for me and welcomed me with a warm smile. Although it was fairly busy, an available agent in business dress and with a compelling smile beckoned me right in. Another agent approached me with a bottle of water, commenting that I must be thirsty after my flight. My reservation was quickly located (an economy car with no frills), and the paperwork was started. I sipped my water and relaxed, just a bit.

At this point, I typically go into *no* mode. *No* to their expensive insurance; *no* to the pre-paid gas; *no* to every add-on or extra. But something was different here. They didn't try to scare me into buying their insurance coverage. They did, though, offer to let me upgrade to a beautiful new SUV (I'd been dying to test drive!) for just $5.00 per day. I heard myself saying *yes*. Then, they proposed that I probably wouldn't want to go through the hassle of stopping in downtown Chicago on the way back to buy gas, when I could relax and let them handle it by prepaying. Another *yes*. And, instead of stopping to pay tolls every 10 miles, it was explained that I could cruise right past them at 65 mph if I purchased their Easy Pass unit. *YES!*

In the end, not only did I spend an extra $120 (out of my own pocket, not expensed), I came away feeling good about the company, the entire transaction, and myself! They had crafted for me an experience that dissolved my defenses and allowed me to open up and be more receptive to options I really did want, but didn't want to be pressured into buying!

That experience was so different from what I expected and what their competitors were offering; I was stunned. They profited nicely by getting me out of *no* mode into saying *yes*. More than that, they earned all my future business, at least until the point where their service falls below my new expectations. Barring that, I'm a customer for life.

Now, what did it cost them to deliver an exceptional experience to me? Add it up:

- Employees who were friendly and dressed in business attire: $0
- Smiles all around: $0
- A bottle of water: $0.30

Yet, giving attention to me as a customer and understanding what I might be feeling and experiencing as I walked into their office earned them a substantial reward—my loyalty and additional purchases. And none of this had to do with what might be construed as their product, the car. In reality, it had everything to do with their real value-add—customer attention and service.

Not all customer experiences are that positive. A friend of mine, a well-known sales trainer, had a different experience. He purchased a brand new home sometime back. The purchase went smoothly, but upon moving in my friend was ready to add some features to his new home—a pool, pool house, garage, landscaping, and finishing the basement.

The problem was that his builder had received his check and moved on, never even asking if there was anything else he could do to add value to my friend's home or lifestyle. And in so doing, he missed out on several thousand dollars of easy additional profit and so wasn't even considered for future jobs. That builder made a sale, but lost a customer.

What will it take to impress your customers with an exceptional customer experience? What will it be worth to you if you do? Ask yourself these questions:

- Who are my customers, and what are they feeling when they enter my office or visit my website?
- What are their pains, fears, uncertainties, or doubts?
- What will they experience from my competitors?
- What are their hopes versus their expectations?
- How can I demonstrate an interest in them above and before an interest in their business?
- How can I create an experience that makes people want to do business with me?

It's not about your product; it's about your concern for your customer first. Enterprise strategically crafted an experience that made me feel good as a person first. By doing that, they earned a customer for life.

As business owners and sales professionals (and that should include all of us), do we make that same mistake by focusing on the *transaction* instead of the *customer*?

Throughout the entire marketing and sales process, you've been building rapport and trust with a customer-centric message and the actions to back it up. You've made it all about them (your customers) and their needs. You've made the sale; that's really where the relationship *starts*!

The most successful retailers in the world know that the first transaction is merely the *opening* transaction. If you do your job and keep a long-term perspective, there will be many more to follow.

Customer Retention and Lifetime Value

There are only four ways to grow your business:

- Get new customers.
- Get customers to buy from you more often.
- Get more customers to spend more money when they buy.
- Get old customers to buy again.

While you spend so much time generating new leads, the fact is that it costs *5–8 times less* to generate revenue from an existing customer than to find a new one. All your marketing and acquisition costs were absorbed in the first sale, so with every subsequent sale your profit margin increases. You've already invested heavily to convert the customer, why not find additional ways to service him and keep him coming back?

Apartment developers and lease communities understand this concept. Keeping residents happy and in place is a community's primary focus. But most retailers, in my experience, don't think in terms of repeat business. After all, selling a home isn't like selling a loaf of bread; the customer won't be back for another one next week. However, there are other ways to keep servicing existing customers, such as maintenance agreements, annual inspections, seasonal service, etc.

For example, according to a recent CNN report, drivers are no longer trading in their new cars every 2–3 years. Rather, the average new car will stay in the buyer's driveway for 11.4 years.[14] That's longer than people used to remain in their homes! That's bad news for automobile manufactures, but just fine for dealerships.

Many are shocked to learn that an automobile dealership makes only a small percentage of their overall profits on new car sales. It's true; the biggest profit points are the service department and the parts department. To the auto dealer, the car purchase is merely the opening transaction in a long-term series of upsells and resells.

Taking a page from the auto dealer's handbook, what can you offer your customers to keep them coming back on a regular basis? The more value you can offer your customers, the greater the lifetime value will be to you and your bottom line. Use the simple calculator in figure 4.1 help you get started.

FIGURE 4.1 Customer lifetime value calculation

Lifetime Value Calculation			
	Segment 1	Segment 2	Segment 3
Average Revenue Per Job			
Average Number of Jobs Per Year	x	x	x
Average Number of Years as a Customer	x	x	x
Total Lifetime Revenue Value of Each Customer	=	=	=

Upsells Add Value and Profits

As previously stated, the first transaction should be viewed as the opening transaction, the beginning of a long and mutually beneficial relationship. In fact, the upsell should begin as soon as the first transaction commences.

Take Amazon as an example. Pick an item, any item, and go to the product page. What do you see? As expected, there are the details of the product, the price, and a big "Add To Cart" button. But look down toward the bottom of the page. The upsell has already begun!

But the way Amazon does it makes perfect sense. If you buy a generator, for example, you're likely to need a heavy-duty extension cord, a cover to protect it, a handle, and wheel kit to move it, etc. They know that the easiest time for them to sell you is when you've got your credit card in your hand and are committed to

4. Number of Transactions

© 2014

making the purchase. And, shoppers who take advantage of the upsells not only spend more, but they are happier, more satisfied customers. They aren't thinking about what the wheel kit cost; they're thinking how easy it is to move the generator anywhere they want without hurting their back!

So, what is *your* next transaction, your upsell? Chances are you already know the items your customers are purchasing within the first few months of moving into their new home. But if not, do this: Picture your customer having just moved into his new home. See him with his family in the home going about his daily activities. Picture him outside, looking at the lawn and landscaping and walking around the house. What is he doing? What does he need? How can you help him make his new home more comfortable, more like *home*?

Like my friend mentioned earlier, perhaps pools or basement finishes are popular. Or maybe landscaping packages are in demand. Before the home is delivered, do you offer upgraded HVAC, insulation, or window packages? Is there an extended warranty that can protect their investment and offer greater peace of mind? Remember, if an item or service adds real value to their home or lifestyle, then you're offering an appreciated service by helping them get it.

Referral Sales—The 'Holy Grail' of Customer Lifetime Value

Word-of-mouth advertising, referrals, are the foundation that every successful business is built upon. If you can do just two things: a) get consistent referral sales and b) manage your overhead and costs effectively, your business is virtually assured of success. Why?

To earn referral sales, everything else in your business must be focused on satisfying your buyers—your sales conversions, pricing, service, everything! You must have high rapport and trust for your buyer to risk their reputation by recommending you. And if you have that, you should be seeing a minimum of 30–40% of your overall sales coming from referrals.

If you have that reputation and emotional capital with your buyers or residents and are *not* seeing strong referrals, then you're bleeding profits that you should be putting into your pocket.

Referrals are your very best sales, your ideal residents. Here's why:

- Happy customers refer people like themselves—people of similar quality and caliber;
- Happy residents refer people they want as neighbors.
- Benefits:
- Virtually no investment in marketing or advertising
- More likely to convert into a buyer
- More realistic expectations
- Fewer problems

Building a Referral Strategy

Increasing the percentage of referral sales requires three things:

1. Measure and record your current referrals as a percentage of overall sales
2. Set specific goals as to where you want your referrals to be
3. Create your strategy, processes, and program to reach your referral goals
   First, determine and record your current referral sales as:

Total Sales: _____ ÷ Referral Sales: _____ = _____

Example: "Total Sales: 10 ÷ Referral Sales: 2 = . 2 or 20%"

Then, set new referral goals:

Increase referrals from _____% to _____% of total sales.

Example: "Increase referrals from 20% to 40% of total sales."

And finally, create and outline your strategy to reach those goals:

Example:

Goal: Increase referrals from 20% to 40% of total sales.

Process: Customer Loyalty/Referral Program

Budget: $80 per customer per year ($80 × 50 = $4,000/yr.)

Steps: 1. Customer Satisfaction Survey

2. Address Key Issues

3. Ensure satisfied customers

4. Define scope of loyalty services

    a. Happy move-in anniversary gift

    b. Seasonal gift/promotions

    c. Community improvement programs

    d. Annual complimentary inspection

5. Define scope of program

    a. Incentives

    b. Referral offer

    c. Time frame

6. Launch program

7. Evaluate and adjust

As an example, I worked with a builder in North Carolina, Jock Tysinger, who held a pig roast every year. Every person Jock ever built a home for was invited to the annual event. Also invited was every prospect that Jock had in his database—everyone that he knew of that he could possibly sell a home to. It was not uncommon for 400–500 guests to attend.

During the dinner, Jock made sure that all his guests were happy and well cared for. His job would be to carve up the pig, serve his guests, and show his appreciation for their patronage. He also made sure every prospect was seated next to a past or current customer. And that's all.

No sales pitch was ever made; no call to action or 'act now and receive at no extra charge' plea was heard. But every year, within a week of the event, Jock would book 15–20 new sales. His customers always came to the dinner with pictures of their homes and stories about how great Jock's service was. They didn't need to be prodded; they were sincerely happy customers and their endorsements were completely honest and unsolicited. They sold the new prospects, not Jock or his sales team. That kind of loyalty has to be earned, but that's what a loyalty program can do for you too.

Anatomy of a Loyalty/Referral Program

As illustrated by Jock's story, your customers are loyal to you when you're loyal to them. It's up to you to keep in touch with them and keep the relationship going. In fact, your loyalty program is made up of just two elements: communication and appreciation. Observe how this is demonstrated in the example below:

Example:

Loyalty Program Outline

Contract signing:	Personal 'Thank You' gift (wine and cheese basket, etc.)
During construction:	Weekly photos and updates of the home-showing progress
At Move-in:	Move-in gift (bring coffee, juice, and breakfast items the morning of)
Each Spring:	Send flower seeds to plant
Each Autumn:	Courtesy inspection; complimentary gutter clean-out; ready for winter
Anniversary:	Wedding or move-in anniversary, send a card and appropriate gift
Holidays:	Cards or small gift, as appropriate
Marketing events:	Include invitations to all past and current buyers

In this example, the appreciation and rapport continued with unexpected service during construction (i.e., weekly photo updates) and never stopped. After move-in, how many times per year did you count a contact or communication? We counted 6–8 touches. And how much do you think that cost? Depending on your circumstances and clientele, an average of $75–$150 would be ample.

Now, what are the rewards? You stay in the front of each customer's mind, and each one considers you as a friend because that's how they've been treated! And having earned their loyalty and appreciation for the continued relationship, don't you think that they'll look for ways to repay you by endorsing you? They will recommend you without reservation to their closest friends and family, knowing that you'll extend the same service and treatment to those whom they refer to you.

When I owned a homebuilding business, we would track young, growing families. On the third anniversary of their purchase, we would go to their homes with a fruit basket. We'd thank them for buying a Strauss home and casually ask, "By the way, how many children do you have now? What is the job situation? Etc." From the contact, we would ask if they were interested in moving "up" or if they could provide referrals. We generated 2–3 sales a year that way with hardly any cost.

Referral Compensation

Which brings us to another often-asked question: Should I pay a referral fee, and if so, how much should it be?

Again, we're talking about showing appreciation. When they hand-deliver a sale to you, that is certainly worthy of appreciation. Interestingly, however, recent studies have shown that most loyal customers feel a bit 'tainted' by accepting a referral fee, as if their endorsement seems less sincere if they are paid for it. They love to be shown appreciation, but in a more honest way than accepting a check.

Here's an alternative: One thing most new homeowners don't have enough of is landscaping or shade trees. So, what if instead of paying them off with a check (see, it even sounds dirty), they heard a knock on the door and opened to find your landscaper with a beautiful maple tree ready to plant? Every time they look at that tree, for as long as they are in that home, they think of the kindness you showed in surprising them with that beautiful tree—not of the transaction for the referral.

Now, we're not saying that a maple tree is the appreciation gift you should always give; that's just an example. The point is that if you find some other way to show real appreciation, something other than a transaction fee, you will build better rapport and relationships with your customers, and they will feel completely uninhibited about referring you to their friends.

When you have a powerful customer loyalty program focused on achieving high levels of customer satisfaction along with a formalized referral program, you can expect an average of five referral sales over the lifetime of every customer.

Calculating Total Customer Lifetime Value

Here's where a change in perspective can help you formulate strategies that move your company to a whole new level of prosperity. The *customer lifetime value* is the cumulative sum of every transaction stemming from a single buyer and can be calculated as:

Average initial sale	_____	+
Average additional sales	_____	+
(Ave. transaction × number of transactions)		
Referral sales	_____	=
Total lifetime revenue	_____	−
Acquisition and service costs	_____	=
Customer lifetime value	_____	

Let's take these one by one. The average initial sale is your average delivered price. You determine that by adding all you sales in a given year and dividing that sum by the number of sales.

Average additional sales refers to the average add-on or delivered sales after the initial sale. If you sold a home and then added a porch or landscaping, that's an additional sale. Keep track of this number and divide it by the total number of sales you make each year.

Referral sales is where the number can become staggering. In the course of their lifetime, on average, how many sales will each homebuyer refer to you? If you track that number closely, you could see four, five, or even more referral sales from each sale you make. This is where fortunes are made!

Add those together to achieve your total lifetime revenue for each customer you acquire. Subtract the costs of marketing, selling, and your loyalty program and you arrive at your customer lifetime value.

If you're not calculating this and measuring it, then you won't see that number grow. But if you watch that number like a hawk, you'll find additional ways to add value to your customers and, in return, to your bottom line.

Creating Your Retention Strategy

As you've seen illustrated with each of the previous Key Numbers, your goal statement should follow this formula:

_____ _____ from _____ to _____ by _____.
    (Verb)   (Noun)   (Number) (Number)   (Date)

The verb is usually increase, decrease, or maintain. In this case, your goal statement might be:

Increase customer retention rate from 60% to 80% by June 1.

Create Strategies

In order to meet this goal, we will:

_____ _____ by _____, _____, & _____.
   (Verb)   (Noun)   by   (Action)   (Action)   and   (Action)

As an example, maybe after reviewing your pricing approach and margins you determine that you want to increase your margins by increasing your prices. Your strategy might be:

Increase our retention rate by implementing a customer loyalty program, creating referral campaigns and hosting an annual customer appreciation dinner.

Once you've identified strategies (the "how you are going to achieve your goal"), it is time to create action plans. Action plans are a numbered list of required tasks. Each task has four components: task name, responsible party, due date, and completion status.

Once you've completed your action plan, you should evaluate the strategy's costs, effectiveness, and return on investment.

Another important component of both profit and cash flow is your pricing. This will be discussed in the next chapter.

5

Pricing your Homes for Profit (#5 of 7)

The fifth of the 7 Key Numbers relates to pricing. Good estimating is the key to good pricing. But, one of the main problems I find is a lack of understanding of this relationship as well as confusion between *markup* and gross margin. A failure to understand this difference can lead to a lack of cash flow and create a need for more work than is necessary.

There's a big difference between market price and profit. But done correctly, you can have both. Profitability comes from understanding the difference between cost, markup, and margin. Most business owners get this one wrong! We'll show you why and how to become more profitable immediately.

Optimal Pricing

Pricing is one of the most important decisions you can make. You probably heard the joke about the company that sold their product for a loss, but still had a huge sale because the CEO thought they could make it up on volume. If you lose $100 each sale, selling 1,000 units only means you lose $100,000! And selling a million units? If you find yourself in a hole, stop digging!

The fact is that most builders get into pricing trouble, not because of faulty marketing, but because of faulty math! Why do builders get their numbers wrong? Partly because there are actually two types of costs involved in the pricing decision:

- The actual hard costs of the product
- The costs that are paid when the product is sold (i.e., commissions, credit card charges, etc.)

Careful consideration of these costs will help you make wiser pricing decisions, whatever your marketing strategy. However, here is a marketing tip for you: price based on value, not based on your competition!

"But," you may thinking, "my customers are very price sensitive! If I am too expensive, I'll lose out to my competitors." If your competition is losing money, do you really want to follow them? As we showed with Art Vandelay, there is something to be said about focusing only on higher value jobs, even if it means forgoing a lot of smaller jobs.

Also, it is impossible to always be the price leader. Don't believe me? Think about Wal-Mart. Definitely low prices. But sometimes you can find things lower price at Target or Costco or even Amazon.com. Even then, Walmart normally doesn't sell things for a loss. They buy so many of every item, their costs are lower than most other retailers. And they may sell for prices that are just a few cents over their (total) cost, but the items are still generating profits. In that case, volume does help. Until you get to the size of Wal-Mart, our advice is to focus on understanding your costs and not on being the price leader.

Pricing Starts With a Good Estimate

If your pricing has to be higher than your costs, what are your costs? It's one thing to know your cost after you incur them. But that doesn't help you much if you have to get your customer to agree to the project or buy the home before you complete the work. You need to be able to predict your costs ahead of time. Of course, we call that an estimate.

An estimate is really a best-guess list of all the costs you will incur in each step of the project with some profit margin built in. The estimate is first step in the 5 C's—you are creating a benchmark that will be your guide through the whole construction process. It is not as complicated as many people think. And, if done right, it actually becomes much easier and more accurate over time.

Just like going to the grocery store, the first step is to make a list of what you need. In construction, your costs are based on the job—job costs. We'll discuss them more in a bit because they are so critical to preparing the estimate.

The second step is to gather quantities. Again, if you are going to shop at the grocery store to buy ingredients for a recipe, you probably know you need a pound of this, a pint of that, and eight ounces of that. In construction, your "recipes" are the architect's plans. Based on them and/or a visit to the job site, you can determine the key quantities to count or measure:

- Foundation requirements
- Wall lengths
- Ceiling geometry
- Appurtenances—windows, doors, lighting accessories, plumbing accessories, floor type, interior/exterior wall covering, roofing material, etc.
- Labor hours required

The third step is to assign unit costs to quantities. Usually, this is simply materials plus labor for each of the steps in the job. If you are subcontracting out some of the work, obtain your prices from subcontractors. As a check, you can look at national job cost data, computer programs, lumber and hardware stores, etc. to get a better idea as to whether your costs are in line with what they should be.

After you list what you will need and how many and how much each item costs, the next step is to crunch the numbers. The sum of (Quantity × Unit Price) for each component is the job cost. The good news is that these can be calculated automatically in any spreadsheet. So, this step should be very easy.

So far, so good. But, the next step is where many people start to go astray: estimating overhead and profit. This helps you calculate your markup to ensure you receive sufficient profit margin to cover your direct costs and overhead, marketing and financing costs.

Wait. Aren't markup and profit margin the same thing? No! Markup is profit margin *divided by* the *cost of goods sold (COGS)*. Don't worry; we'll explain it in detail below. But for now, a word of caution: you may be tempted to cut your margins to be competitive. Don't win the job and lose your company.

Create your Job-Cost Codes

Let's talk more about job costs and job-cost codes. You prime your estimating system by creating your job-cost and job-billing codes. (Yes, a process, a system!) This is simply a process of breaking down a job into smaller components through which you can track costs. If you are a homebuilder, the National Association of Home Builders has a standard chart of accounts. You can use that or use your own. In any event, the "code" is simply a way to differentiate and organize your job costs.

You use these codes to identify each major category or milestone involved in completing your project. And for each major category, you then create steps within the category. The smaller the steps the better, as every step in the process has the potential to cost you more than you get paid for it. The more you track, the more you control your costs. But there is a limit. I had a builder suggest 6,548 cost codes. For the life of me, I can't figure out how you can manage that many. In this case, we paired it down to 38 (no joke). Make sure the number of codes is manageable to ensure consistency. On average, consider between 50 and 125 maximum.

The estimate in figure 5.1 is for other onsite costs. In other words, options the homeowner wants added to the home. You can see that this is simply a list of costs you'd incur building these options and their associated costs. And, because this is all part of the same category, they all have the same job-cost code, 500.

More generally, cost codes are a list of "activities." For instance, here are our primary activities in building a home:

- Preparation and preliminaries
- Excavation and foundation
- Rough structure
- Full enclosure
- Finishing trades
- Completion and inspection
- Indirect costs

This list was adapted from the National Association of Homebuilders' Chart of Accounts, and each industry may have its own structure. Now, each of these activities or categories of activities can be further broken down into sub-activities (or as

FIGURE 5.1 Other onsite costs

Please enter the details of the Job Estimate. Bold fields are required.

| Save and Close | Save and New | Cancel | | Markup %: 35.00 | | Apply Markup % To All | | Copy Another Job Estimate... | ▼ | Create Job... |

Job Estimate

ID			500		Name							Other Onsite Costs	
Item No.	G/L Acct.	Job Cost	Job Billing Description		Quantity	Per Unit	Total Cost	Markup $	Markup %	Total Billing	Allowances	Grand Total
	5100	500	ABS Pad				400.00	140.00	35.00	540.00		540.00
	5100	500	All 32 W				2,900.00	1,015.00	35.00	3,915.00		3,915.00
	5100	500	Awning - Extend Gable				150.00	52.50	35.00	202.50		202.50
	5100	500	Awning 8x20				650.00	227.50	35.00	877.50		877.50
	5100	500	Block up 28' under 66'				2,700.00	945.00	35.00	3,645.00		3,645.00
	5100	500	Cooler 13 Seer 2.0 Ton				2,904.00	1,016.40	35.00	3,920.40		3,920.40
	5100	500	Cooler 13 Seer 2.5 Ton				3,012.00	1,054.20	35.00	4,066.20		4,066.20
	5100	500	Cooler 13 Seer 3.0 Ton				3,120.00	1,092.00	35.00	4,212.00		4,212.00
	5100	500	Cooler 13 Seer 3.5 Ton				3,180.00	1,113.00	35.00	4,293.00		4,293.00
	5100	500	Cooler 13 Seer 4.0 Ton				3,216.00	1,125.60	35.00	4,341.60		4,341.60
	5100	500	DW 60' or less				815.00	285.25	35.00	1,100.25		1,100.25
	5100	500	Fiberglass step w/ rail				235.00	82.25	35.00	317.25		317.25
	5100	500	Labor				600.00	210.00	35.00	810.00		810.00
	5100	500	Metal - 8x10				800.00	280.00	35.00	1,080.00		1,080.00
	5100	500	MOD under 61' (no crane)				4,200.00	1,470.00	35.00	5,670.00		5,670.00
	5100	500	OtherDW over 60'				920.00	322.00	35.00	1,242.00		1,242.00
	5100	500	Sheds - Heartland 8x10				1,700.00	595.00	35.00	2,295.00		2,295.00
	5100	500	Sheds - Standard Wood 8x10				1,100.00	385.00	35.00	1,485.00		1,485.00

we call them: parents and children). For instance, full enclosure might include the following "children" accounts, or sub-activities:

- Roofing
- Masonry
- Windows/exterior doors
- Overhead garage door
- Insulation

Similarly, we can list "children" for all the major cost codes, including preparation & preliminaries, excavation & foundation, rough structure, etc., to truly map out all the expected costs going out door. What about the other side of the ledger—money coming in?

Creating your Job-Billing Codes

How can you manage your billings to improve your cash flow? Use billing costs to schedule when your customer has to pay you to cover specific costs.

Billing codes ensure you get paid for reaching certain milestones. This ensures consistent cash flow, which is one of the critical principles of profitability. (It also helps you know much sooner if you have a problem customer.) You can set up your billing codes to reflect a payment schedule (if you do progress billing) or a base price plus change orders. For example, if you have your job-cost codes set up, you might notice that you will incur a lot of costs getting started. This may include getting permits and buying materials you will need immediately. Wouldn't it be nice to get some money from your customer to cover those costs so you aren't spending *your* cash and exposing your business to unnecessary risk from the negative cash flow? You can. Assign a bill code, perhaps "Deposit," to those job-cost codes so you can bill your client for that set of costs.

You really can have complete flexibility to ensure your billing codes adhere to your cash flow requirements and profitability goals. Improving your cash flow is critical to your company's ability to survive. But it also helps your profitability. Think about this: if you have predictable and consistent cash flow, you may not need to secure large loans with hefty interest payments.

Create a Worksheet to Estimate

Estimating is a form of *management by objective*, which implies that objectives will be established, quantified, and then broken down into sub-goals (standards of performance).

FIGURE 5.2 Blank job estimate worksheet

							Job Estimate				
							Name				
Job Cost	Job Billing	Description					Quantity	Per Unit	Total Cost	Markup $	Markup %	Total Billing
												0.00
												0.00
												0.00
												0.00
												0.00
							Add Detail				

An estimate is a guess. Not the sophisticated definition you were expecting? The truth is, many people get hung up over-thinking this. It doesn't have to be perfect at first.

In the sample worksheet in figure 5.2, you have cost codes, billing codes, quantities, percent costs, the total cost, and a markup. Figure 5.3 shows the spreadsheet with the estimate information filled in.

FIGURE 5.3 Spreadsheet with estimate information filled in

Job Cost Code	Job Billing	Description	Quantity	Per Unit	Total Cost
803	1000	20 yard roll of dumpster. Per dump.	3	304.17	912.50
803	1000	Demo existing kitchen: Contractor will remove cabinets, counter tops, sink and appliances. Contractor will demo sift, open chase, apply coverings to existing floors to	1	2,133.33	2,133.33
803	1000	Mask work area at doorway openings. Includes masking materials up to $150.	1	350.00	350.00
Total 803 - Demo					3,395.83
805	1000	Back out framing. Blocking and cripples for backing on walls and drywall.	1	200.00	200.00
805	1000	Construct walls for new "Laundry" location.	14	20.00	280.00
805	1000	Drop ceiling in kitchen and living room to match ceiling height in "sun space" requires	1	280.00	280.00
Total 805 - Framing					4,060.00

The "Production Cycle Approach" to Healthy Cash Flow

Picture this: your phones are ringing, your orders are piling up, your people are working at full capacity, and your P&L shows a nice, healthy profit. Good times, right? Except there's a problem: you don't have enough cash to cover payroll. Which means it's all going to come grinding to a halt.

How can you avoid this "death by indigestion instead of starvation"? As we have been discussing, the solution is to accurately identify when you spend money related to each job. You do this by taking inventory of all the steps in your production cycle (from writing proposals to buying raw materials to paying for hourly labor) and the related cash outflows. Then, once you know where your cash is flowing out at each point in your production cycle, you should compare to where your cash is flowing in.

Look at table 5.1. It shows the normal timing for how most businesses spend and receive cash.

TABLE 5.1 Timing of cash outflows and inflows

	Cash Outflows	Cash Inflows
Acquiring leads	5%	0%
Closing the lead	5%	0%
Completing the sale	5%	0%
Construction	70%	60%
Punch list & Completion	15%	40%
Warranty and follow-up	100%	100%

See the problem here? By the end of the job, after you've already delivered (or distributed) the final product, you've incurred 90% of your costs but you've only received 60% of your revenue. And you've probably got to wait another 30 or 60 days beyond the completion of your follow-up activities to receive that last check. You're funding your customer.

If your table shows a similar pattern, then your revenue cycle is not strategically aligned with your production cycle. Your cash flow is out of balance. One solution is to create multiple payment milestones earlier in your production cycle. Instead of doing the work for them before they pay you, we want you to create a progress billing schedule so that you give them work *after* they give you money.

How does that sound to you? Think about how restaurants operate. When you dine in at a restaurant, they give you the food and then you pay (maybe 30 minutes later). However, when you order take out, you pay them before they hand you your food. Essentially the same transaction, but the timing is different. In this case, it's only a difference of 30 minutes. But what is your time frame? How long does it take you to do the work and get paid? By using billing codes, you can greatly help align your cash inflow and cash outflow, generally without even raising an eyebrow from your customer.

Determining your Ideal Selling Price

OK, so we've discussed how to better identify your standard costs. Now, let's talk about the next step: figuring out how much to charge your customer.

As a CPA with decades of experience in the homebuilding industry, I've seen too many business owners lose their shirts by underpricing their products. Sure, there are times when you might cut profits by offering incentives to move inventory. And you have to be priced according to your market; clench-fisted buyers won't pay a penny more than they have to and are likely to negotiate ferociously. But, as I said before, the fact is that most builders get into pricing trouble, not because of faulty marketing, but because of faulty math!

The key to arriving at your ideal price—one that keeps you out of the red—is to realistically calculate these three things: cost, commissions, and profit margin.

I will go through the steps of how to accurately calculate each of these—particularly commissions and profits. Let's say that a house will cost you $300,000 to build. What is the ideal selling price for that house? Do you have a sales team that you pay on commission? If so, then you need to accurately calculate the price of the home including your commissions. Sounds simple enough, but too many smart business owners get this wrong.

Problem 1: Calculating Cost + Commissions

For the sake of argument (and because the math is simple), suppose you pay a whopping 10% commission. Easy! You just add 10% onto the cost to make sure you cover your commission fees. Doing the math, 10% of $300,000 is $30,000.

So, what if you just add $30,000 to the cost of the house and sell it for $330,000? There are two problems with that. First, the percentage should be taken off the top, *not* added to the bottom. You are paying 10% commission on the *sale* price of $330,000. So the math should be: 10% of $330,000 is $33,000, *not* $30,000. This means you won't cover your costs! If you sell the house for $330,000 and deduct the 10% commission ($33,000), you are left with only $297,000. That's less than the cost of $300,000, so you just went in the hole by $3,000. And, your sales person just got paid a handsome $33,000, so they'll keep selling these homes as quickly as they can, putting you $3,000 deeper in the hole each time. Make it up on volume? No. The bigger the volume, the bigger the problem!

Problem 2: Calculating Cost + Commissions + Profits

This brings us to the second problem: your margins or gross profit. You aren't trying to just break even on the job; you want some profit, don't you? If your target is 25% gross profit margin on each job, and it costs $300,000 to build, many people will simply add 25% of $300,000 ($75,000) to the cost and try to sell the house for $375,000.

This has the same problem we just discussed. Doing the math, 25% of $375,000 is $93,750. If you sell the house for $375,000, you'll only make the $75,000 difference over your costs, which is only 20%. This is short of your 25% target by $18,750!

So, how do you account for these percentage costs? How do you really price for commission and profit margins? You need to understand the difference between markup and a cost multiplier. Let me explain each term and the difference between them so you are more comfortable with the concepts.

Pricing with Markup and/or Gross Profit

I like to keep things simple. And, I'm hungry. So let's use an example about bananas to explain the difference. Imagine you buy a banana for a dollar, and you sell it for two dollars. (Hey, Starbucks does it every day!) You marked it up $1.00 and made exactly $1.00 profit. Easy stuff, right?

There's a deep dark hole that many business owners fall into when trying to determine profit as a percentage of sales. Markup does *not* equal profit (except maybe in bananas!). But, in the banana example, even though both are $1 in absolute terms, the markup is 100% and profit is 50%. Markup and profit margin are percentages. Markup is based on cost; profit margin is based on revenue.

Particularly for contractors and builders, it's vital to understand the relationship between gross profit, job cost as a percentage of sales, and markup. The most important thing to remember is that if you know your gross profit or your job-cost percentage, you can easily figure out how much of a markup you need for your products. They are all related.

First and foremost, determine your *gross profit* goal. How many dollars do you want to "take home" as profit? This leads to the next question: how much of a markup do you need to add to your products? Look at your company's gross profit goal. And remember, gross profit should include your overhead costs as well as your ideal net profit. In other words, the amount of markup you shoot for is dependent upon your overhead structure and the profit goal you have. The overhead costs should include all salaries, including your own, plus all costs associated with running a first class operation. Table 5.2 indicates the relationship between gross profit, job costs, and markup.

Let's look at these in turn. For every dollar you earn in revenue, some goes toward your costs and some, let's hope, is profit. Since there are only the two categories, the two numbers are related. As you see in the first row of the table, if 80% of the sale price is used to cover job costs, that leaves 20% for gross profit. (If you make a dollar and it cost you $.80, your gross profit is $.20, right?)

TABLE 5.2 Gross profit, job costs, and markup

To Achieve this Gross Profit (%)	as a % of Sales	Job Costs Costs by This %	Markup Cost Multiplier
20.0	80.0	25.0	1.25
25.0	75.0	33.3	1.33
30.0	70.0	42.9	1.43
33.3	66.7	50.0	1.50
35.0	65.0	53.8	1.54
40.0	60.0	66.7	1.67
42.9	57.2	75.0	1.75
45.0	55.0	81.8	1.82
50.0	50.0	100.0	2.00
Formula:	1 − (col 1)	(col 1) ÷ (col 2)	1 + (col 3)

$$\text{Price} - \text{Cost} = \text{Gross Profit}$$

$$\text{Price} - \text{Gross Profit} = \text{Cost}$$

But what if you knew your costs are $.80 and you wanted to figure out how to price it so you can generate $.20 in profit? The Markup Cost Multiplier column tells us how to do that. Let's keep the same numbers. It's easy to see that the $.80 in costs plus $.20 in profit means your price is $1.00. So, you are marking up the $.80 by $.20, which is 25% of that $.80. The general equation is:

Profit ÷ Job Costs = Markup Percentage

Since most people don't like division, the cost multiplier turns it into a multiplication problem. If you know your costs are $.80 and you want a profit of $.20, multiple that $.80 by 1.25 to calculate your ideal price. This all works nicely, whatever your cost structure and profit goals.

So, how do you account for percent costs—those like commission and profit margins that add to, yet come from, your sales price? The math is a little different, but still not too difficult.

$$\text{Price} = \text{Cost} \div (1 - \text{Percentage})$$

Assume that the home costs $300,000 to build, you pay a 6% commission, and you want a 20% gross profit margin. If you were just calculating the sales commission, the formula would be:

$$\text{Price} = \$300{,}000 \div (1 - 06\%) = \$300{,}000 \div .94 = \$319{,}149$$

(To double check, calculate 6% of $319,149 ($319,149 × .06 = $19,149), then subtract it from the total ($319,149 – $19,149 = $300,000).Yes!) But you need to add in the 20% margin as well. Use the same formula, but first calculate the total percentage you need to factor in is 20% (margin) + 6% (commission) = 26%.

$$Price = \$300,000 \div (1 - 26\%) = \$405,405.$$

(Again, to double check: $405,405 × .26 = $105,405. So your Total Costs: $405,405 – $105,405 = $300,000.

As you can see the ideal price is $405,405. Can you imagine charging a client this amount? You don't need to charge exactly this amount, but this is the ideal price to meet your goals. You could round it up to $405,900 (and make an extra $495) or offer a reduced price of $404,999 to meet market expectations with the knowledge that your margins will be $406 less than your target. But, now you are pricing from a position of strength.

Putting It All Together

Look at the example in figure 5.4. You can see the job-cost codes to the left of each item and the markup on the right. The markup on every item is 20%. After you add all the costs, you arrive at a total cost of $4,060. With the 20% markup, the total billing (or price) is $4,872.

FIGURE 5.4 Job costs and markup

G/L Acct.	Job Cost Code	Job Billing	Description	Quantity	Per Unit	Total Cost	Mark up $	Markup %	Total Billing
5100	801	1400	Remodel kitchen based off plan sketches provided by contractor. Final estimate will be provided after final architectural plans are provided, unforeseen conditions will change costs.			0.00			0.00
Total 801 - Scope of Work						0.00			0.00
5100	803	1000	20 yard roll of dumpster. Per dump.	3	304.17	912.50	182.50	20	1,095.00
5100	803	1000	Demo existing kitchen: Contractor will remove cabinets, counter tops, sink and appliances. Contractor will demo sift, open chase, apply coverings to existing floors to prevent damage, remove existing tile floor and carpeting. 22 Demo wall between the "Sun Space" and "kitchen/dining room". 8 Demo wall between "Kitchen" and "Dining room". 4 Demo existing ceiling drywall in kitchen and living room areas. Required to fr ceiling down to height of sun space ceiling. 8	1	2,133.33	2,133.33	426.67	20	2,560.00
5100	803	1000	Mask work area at doorway openings. Includes masking materials up to $150.	1	350.00	350.00	70.00	20	420.00
Total 803 - Demo						3,395.83			4,075.00
5100	805	1000	Back out framing. Blocking and cripples for backing on walls and drywall.	1	200.00	200.00	40.00	20	240.00
5100	805	1000	Construct walls for new "Laundry" location.	14	20.00	280.00	56.00	20	336.00
5100	805	1000	Drop ceiling in kitchen and living room to match ceiling height in "sun space"	1	280.00	280.00	56.00	20	336.00
5100	805	1000	Materials: Framing materials	1	600.00	600.00	120.00	20	720.00
5100	805	1000	NOTE: scope of work will be finalized after engineering plans have been	2	100.00	200.00	40.00	20	240.00
5100	805	1000	Structural framing for wall removal, supporting 2nd story wall. Rough cost with steel I-beam, steel posts, and footers; rough costs pending structural engineering requirements.	1	2,500.00	2,500.00	500.00	20	3,000.00
Total 805 - Framing						4,060.00			4,872.00

Let's do the calculations we've discussed.

$$\text{Total Cost} \div \text{Price} = \$4,060 \div \$4,872 = 83.33\%$$

$$\text{Price} - \text{Cost} = \text{Gross Profit}$$

$$\text{In dollars, the equation is: } \$4,872 - \$4,060 = \$812$$

$$\text{In percentages, the equation is: } 100\% - 83.33 = 16.67\%$$

Note the profit margin is 16.67% while the markup is 20%.

Do's and Don'ts of Estimating

Besides giving you better information to determine a price that sufficiently covers your cost, a good, detailed bid also demonstrates competence and professionalism. It also helps the client envision both the completed project *and* a positive experience during construction because they know you won't surprise them with extra costs. Furthermore, it holds your superintendents accountable since you can easily tell if they are within budget or over.

How do you ensure a good, detailed estimate? Make sure to analyze it closely. This includes double-checking your work and even comparing your estimate to past jobs. Also, clearly spell out what your bid includes and excludes. It should include allowances, selection details, specifications, finishes, and any special scheduling.

Sound doable? Just remember: don't over-think it. An estimate is just a guess. Also, don't reinvent the wheel if you don't have to. If one estimate is similar to another one you created previously, copy as much of it as you can. And, finally, don't estimate in isolation. Your sales estimate needs to include current cost and needs to be entered into your accounting system once the estimate is approved and accepted. And, after the job is done—if not while the job is in process—compare the estimate to actuals so you can create more accurate estimates in the future.

Do's and Don'ts of Pricing

There are three pricing levers that control a company's profits: price, cost, and sales volume. Unprofitable companies tend to rely on increasing their sales volume. Over the long term, this can have unintended consequences. Profitable companies use all three levers.

Remember to base pricing decisions on hard data. Companies need to understand at a detailed level the factors that drive their customers' purchase decisions. So, develop a data model for making rational price decisions. Understand the various pricing models you can use, but it is preferable to use market-based pricing, not cost-based pricing. Remember, price is what someone will pay. Value is what they receive. You can tailor your prices to different market segments because different customers will value your products and services differently. This is called price discrimination.

First, you'll need to find a segmentation scheme that works and apply it rigorously. Companies should tag every customer and every prospect with market segment tags, so all of their analyses can look at the costs, revenues, and rates of change and profits by market segment. What are their demographics, psychographics and sociographics? What is your buyers' urgency? Understanding these factors can help you price based on value, not cost.

This includes options and upgrades. By definition, they are not your standard product or model. By extension, you believe that only some people will want them. Only those customers will value them. So, you should have this mindset: "The margin on our options will vary depending on their nature and the availability of comparable pricing." If this is something truly valuable and unique, you should be able to add a very comfortable margin.

As we said at the beginning of this section, don't price based on your competition. Do the work to understand your costs and profit margins. Don't take a shortcut and price based on rules of thumb. One more piece of advice: don't rely on your sales people for pricing decisions. Companies should not trust that their sales and marketing people would feed them accurate, un-tainted data. They should find data sources that are more reliable. Remember the example we described above where the sales person received their commission on the $330,000 home, even though the company lost $3,000.

Conclusion

In order to start turning a decent profit and take the first steps to begin thriving, you will need to optimize your average price per transaction. This may mean increasing the price, or it may mean decreasing the price—the decision depends on your pricing strategy.

Basic economics has taught us that as prices go up, demand goes down, and vice versa; but that's not the whole story. In fact, changing your pricing strategy will impact every aspect of your business.

If you raise your prices, for example, you must now target and market to a more affluent clientele than before. This means incurring different (and probably more expensive) marketing and sales costs! Also, because these customers will expect higher quality and service, your labor and materials costs will go up as well. So what good is raising prices if your costs increase along with them?

If, however, you lower prices with the intent of lowering your marketing, sales, and production costs, you may find yourself in a similar bind because you ended up trimming your margins too close to the bone. Essentially, what good is lowering your prices if your margins drop so low that your higher volume won't translate into higher profits?

The point is that your pricing strategy ripples across your entire business. To understand the impact of pricing changes, you can use the *8 P's*.

The 8 P's: The Pillars of your Business

The 8 P's are another way of describing your business funnel. Here's an example of tracking the impact of your pricing strategy across the 8 P's. Let's say you want to raise the average price of your homes from $300,000 to $500,000. How would that impact your other P's?

- **Purpose.** You would probably change your company's mission statement from a focus on "value" to a focus on "luxury."
- **Product.** You would need to consider new designs, materials, layouts, and so on.
- **Place.** The neighborhood you build in would become a lot more important.
- **Price.** You may need to consider new financing options.
- **Promotion.** You will probably need to upgrade your marketing material and retrain your sales staff to speak to the needs of more affluent customers.
- **Production.** You will need to invest a lot more in the way you build your houses.
- **People.** You will probably have to work with new architects, landscapers, designers, and, quite possibly, a fung shui consultant.
- **Profit.** You want to make sure that your profit goals are higher, even after you've incurred increased costs.

When you're considering increasing your prices, it's important to think through the ramifications of that change on the other pillars. Such analysis will help you determine what other aspects of your business you need to shift to make the pricing change work.

This same type of analysis is equally important when lowering prices. It's far too easy to believe that increased volume can overcome the amount you lose per transaction, but volume alone won't solve your problems.

Price for Profit

Every time I considered a price change for my construction business, I didn't merely update the website with the new prices. Instead, I spent half a day with my staff thinking through and discussing all the ramifications of the changes.

Salespeople provide insight into how your customers will react to change. Marketing examines how your message will have to change in order to communicate greater value. The production staff discusses the changes to materials and labor and their related costs that will need to be implemented to meet higher customer expectations. And the financial staff provides insight into how your cost structure will change to accommodate these new inputs.

But you don't need a giant staff to do this. You can draw a simple table with the 8 P's and a few columns for the different price points you are considering. Then, all you have to do is fill in the blanks with how each price change would impact everything down to profit.

I've got one word of caution before you begin, though: don't price for cost, price for profit. If you price for cost, you'll gravitate toward the price that incurs the lowest cost. But if you take everything into consideration when pricing for profit, you'll end up with a price that drives the highest profit and enables you to make real money. Now translate that to goals for estimating and pricing.

Create Goals

To be successful in pricing for profit, you must:

_____ _____ from _____ to _____ by _____.
   (Verb)   (Noun)   (Number) (Number)   (Date)

The verb is usually increase, decrease, or maintain.

Create Strategies

In order to meet this goal, you will:

_____ _____ by _____, _____, & _____.
   (Verb)   (Noun)   by   (Action)   (Action)   and   (Action)

As an example, maybe after reviewing your pricing approach and margins, as well as the 8 P's table, you determine that you want to increase your margins by increasing your prices. A goal setting statement might be:

Increase gross margin from 20% to 40% by June 2015.

Your strategy might be:

Increase our average price by retooling our marketing, training our sales people, and designing more luxurious homes.

Once you've identified strategies (the "how you are going to achieve your goal"), it is time to create action plans. Action plans are a numbered list of required tasks. Each task has four components: task name, responsible party, due date, and completion status.

Once you've completed your action plan, you should evaluate the strategy's costs, effectiveness, and return on investment.

6

Controlling Costs—
The Key to Profitability
(#6 of 7)

In the last chapter, we talked about how to price your work so that you can make a profit. We discussed how many business owners use faulty math and don't give themselves a chance to make money. Now that you know how to price appropriately, how do you ensure that you wind up making money after the job is done? The key is control your costs so they line up with your expectations (i.e., your estimate). In this chapter we are going to talk about variable costs, the sixth of the 7 Key Numbers.

Here are two axioms that you've already seen several times in this book, and we hope you will remember long into the future:

- You can't manage what you don't measure.
- That which you measure tends to improve.

(By the way, that's not only true in business, but in many areas of life. Can you imagine if a sprinter didn't measure their time, a doctor who didn't measure your blood pressure or your cholesterol level, or the teacher who didn't give grades?)

In this part, you'll learn how to accurately measure and manage your costs to increase profitability.

Controlling Your Job Costs

In the construction industry, there are five distinct, but related, phases to control profitability and cash flow:

1. Estimating
2. Scheduling
3. Cost control
4. Change order administration
5. Draw preparation

We covered estimating in depth in Chapter 5. Let's go through the rest one at a time.

Scheduling

Although scheduling is not a part of financial accounting, it is a part of job management and is essential in controlling the progress of a job. How? A schedule is a timetable, which communicates the following information:

- **What must be done?** Almost everything you do has a cost associated to it, doesn't it?
- **When it needs to start?** This helps you control your cash flow.
- **Who needs to do it?** Usually, this means who are you going to pay to do it?
- **How long does it takes?** In other words, how much are you going to pay them to do it?
- **Date when it must be completed?** This helps you be able to plan the next steps.
- **What other tasks depend on it?** This tells you what else you cannot do until this part is done.

Remember, in maintaining our numbers, we want to monitor more than financial results. Every aspect of your business drives profitability and cash flow.

With that in mind, why do you need to create and monitor your schedule? There are two main reasons. The big one is that time is money. This isn't just a common expression, but it is really true. If your vendors are late completing something, you often have to hold up other work; you might be renting equipment or paying other people to be there, and now the next phase is being delayed. And when you are slow to complete the project, it takes longer to get paid. The second main reason for a schedule is to prevent you from paying bills when the work isn't completed. It seems like some vendors have no shame . . . or a lot of nerve. So, you need to be diligent in checking the schedule before you pay their bill. Again, time is money. So, when your vendors are late, it is costing you money. Why not have them pay for the delay instead of you?

These reasons are mostly reactive, catching issues after they arise. A schedule can allow you to be proactive too. You can identify potential problems by knowing what tasks need to be performed, in what order, and when the resources need to be ordered. Can you imagine having the roofers show up before the walls are even erected? Or the masons arriving at the worksite to only then to discover no one ordered the bricks, and they take a week to deliver? If you don't use schedules, then I suspect that these issues may sound rather familiar. With proper schedules, you can actually manage multiple jobs much easier because you can make sure not to allocate the same resources to multiple jobs simultaneously.

Schedules don't just save you money, but they can also help you make more money too. Schedules establish a communication method, providing a means of confirming everyone's expectations. This includes the customers! By letting clients know what to expect, you can greatly improve customer service and satisfaction. Not knowing when a project will finish drives clients insane! As a production builder, I found the same problems delivering houses when promised.

Another competitive advantage of scheduling is that you can easily identify the status of every job status and immediately take corrective action as necessary. You also can continuously hone your systems, preventing delays, and even speeding things up by measuring the schedule. At minimum, you can contact your client immediately if there is a delay so they are not surprised later on.

So, what are the steps in the scheduling process?

- **Define the scope of work.**
- **Create the list of tasks, milestones, durations, and resources.**
- **Cross check with your estimate.** Did you take everything you should have into consideration? The total cost should equate to man hours.
- **Post the schedule** (perhaps on your internal website) and make sure everyone involved in the project knows how to read the schedule. Also, provide reminders to your vendors.
- **Review the schedule frequently.**

That last one is worth repeating. Look at your schedule often to see if you are on time. This way, you can identify vendors who are constantly late or are constantly issuing change orders. You can then decide if you want to continue using them or change how you work with them. In industries that are dominated by subcontracting, this is a very important facet of profitability.

Reviewing your schedule is not complicated. Look at the schedule in figure 6.1 and ask yourself these questions:

- Is my job progressing according to schedule?
- Who is in charge of a particular task (either an employee or a vendor)?
- Are there any notes that I want to keep track of?

FIGURE 6.1 Sample schedule

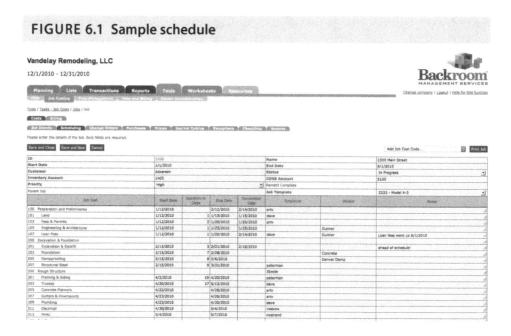

Controlling the Flow of Money

Here's a pretty simple question for you to consider: why is job costing so important? Most people think it is because you want to minimize your costs. However, what does it mean if your costs are zero? It means you're out of business! Costs are like taxes. If you are paying a lot, it should mean you are making more money to begin with.

The reason why job costing is so important is that as your company grows, your cost of goods sold becomes your biggest drain on cash. Why? Because your company is *doing* so much more!

Whether building houses, making other products, operating a retail store, or providing a service, growth means you are busy; you're hopefully busy making money, but also busy adding costs and spending money on things or resources that you will later profit from. And, without control of this important cost center, you stand to lose a lot of money. So the real goal of controlling your costs is to keep them in line with your revenue and growth while not risking either. Builders go out of business $200 at a time.

By comparison, a frequent sign of poor cost control is a contractor who is using a current job's receipts to pay for the last job's bills. That means they'll need to pay for this current job with the *next* job. What if that next job doesn't come soon enough to cover your bills *now*? With cash flow engineering, every job pays for itself and has positive cash flow.

The 5 C's of Financial Management

In the first chapter, you were introduced to the 5 C's of financial management. The first C is to create your benchmarks. In terms of job costs, the benchmark is the estimate (and schedule), which we've discussed. Now let's focus on the next four C's:

- **Collect** meaningful information
- **Compile** data into useful forms
- **Compare** your (actual) results to your expectations (job budgets and pricing)
- **Correct** your trajectory

The 2nd C: Collect Data

If you really think about it, a business does only one of two things:

- Buys things (cash outflows)
- Sells things (cash inflow)

Yes, it is that simple. So job-cost accounting should be simple too. In reality, it only requires your bookkeepers and accountants to:

- track costs to a job and cost code; and
- track receipts to a job and billing code.

3rd C: Compile Data

When we did accounting by hand, this was a major task. You had to determine which reports you needed and then spend countless man hours creating those reports. Today, it is simply a matter of clicking on the correct tabs within your software.

4th C: Compare Data

In this section we are going to talk about managing your jobs. We'll start with an overview, then look at your jobs at a macro or top level in order to isolate jobs that are not performing to our expectations, and then do a deep dive to managing the jobs on a job by job level (the micro level).

Managing Your Jobs

I've been a CPA a long time. If you look at the tax code (which I don't recommend), it changes every year—sometimes more than a couple of times within a year. So, how do I keep up with all the changes? Here's what I learned: Over time, the answers keep changing, but the question remains the same! For instance, is a transaction a capital gain or ordinary income? Well, what constitutes a capital *asset* versus an item subject to ordinary income is constantly changing, but the question has never changed. By the way, don't worry if that example doesn't make sense to you. Why? Business questions haven't changed since the dawn of mankind (i.e., "What do you offer?" or "Who is your target market?" or "How much will you charge, etc.?").

The key is to know what questions to ask and then get the answers. As the business owner, you don't have to be an accountant. Let your bookkeeper collect the data and compile the reports (push the correct buttons). You just have to know how to read them to answer your questions.

Manage by Exception—The Macro View

You need to be able to react to problems, project your costs and your income, and identify your best and worst employees, contractors, and partners.

Our philosophy is that reports don't just show you numbers; they help you answer important questions. Which report you look at depends on what question you are asking:

- Are my jobs on budget? If the answer is no, then why not?
- Am I getting more cash in than I'm paying out?
- Which job or jobs are falling behind? If you have project managers, which one is performing well, who is not?
- Which of my vendors are going over budget? Which are behind schedule?
- What lead sources are bringing me the most business? Which is making me the most money?

You need to be able to look at all your jobs at once or one job at a time. Now, let's look at some examples of common reports you may find useful, whether you create them yourself or generate them from financial software. But more importantly, let's look at questions you should be asking and how the different reports can provide answers.

Job Budget & Costs for Multiple Jobs

This report shows job costs and compares costs to your budgets for every job you selected (fig 6.2). A report like this can help you answer these questions:

FIGURE 6.2 Job budget and costs report

	Job Budget			Job Costs				
Job	Original Estimate	Change Orders	Revised Amount	Previous Costs	Current Costs	Total Costs	Percent Complete	Balance to Finish
1000 - 1000 Main Street	173,877.00	8,810.00	182,487.00	48,500.00	0.00	48,500.00	26.58 %	133,987.00
1001 - 1001 Main Street	173,877.00	500.00	174,377.00	0.00	0.00	0.00	0.00 %	174,377.00
1011 - 101 First Street - HVAC Install	5,525.00	0.00	5,525.00	0.00	0.00	0.00	0.00 %	5,525.00
1012 - 202 Second Street - HVAC Install	5,525.00	0.00	5,525.00	0.00	0.00	0.00	0.00 %	5,525.00
	358,804.00	9,110.00	367,914.00	48,500.00	0.00	48,500.00	13.18 %	319,414.00

Vandelay Remodeling, LLC — Job Budget and Costs — 11/3/2013 8:39:06 AM — Page 1 of 1

- How many jobs are active now (in total or within a group you specify)?
- How much money have you spent in this period on these jobs?
- How much more money will you have to spend to complete them?

Job Profitability

With this report, you can get a snapshot for every job and your company as a whole (fig 6.3). A report like this can help you answer these questions:

- What is the expected profit in each job?
- What is the expected profit for all these jobs?
- Which jobs are over budget and by how much?

FIGURE 6.3 Job profitability report

			Budgeted			Projected			
ID	Name	Type	Revenue	Total Costs	Profit	Revenue	Total Costs	Profit	Variance
1	job from estimate		10,081.25	8,065.00	2,016.25	10,081.25	8,065.00	2,016.25	0.00
1000	1000 Main Street		232,500.00	179,277.00	53,223.00	232,500.00	179,777.00	52,723.00	-500.00
1001	505 Second Ave		230,000.00	171,657.00	58,343.00	230,000.00	171,657.00	58,343.00	0.00
1004	Replace Roof - 123 Main St		21,370.40	17,392.00	3,978.40	21,370.40	17,392.00	3,978.40	0.00
2222	200 Broadway (Model A -3)		210,000.00	181,402.00	28,598.00	210,000.00	181,402.00	28,598.00	0.00
			703,951.65	557,793.00	146,158.65	703,951.65	558,293.00	145,658.65	-500.00

Vandelay Remodeling, LLC — Job Profitability — As Of 12/31/2010 — 12/6/2014 10:32:24 AM — Page 1 of 1

If there are specific questions or issues, you can then go to the job in question to investigate.

Job Profitability Cash Basis

There should be little argument that knowing how each job is doing compared to its budget is important. Knowing your current and pending billing opportunities and cost obligations is critical to managing your cash flow (fig. 6.4).

FIGURE 6.4 Job profitability cash basis report

Vandelay Remodeling, LLC

12/6/2014 10:34:30 AM

Job Profitability Cash Basis

As Of 12/31/2010

Page 1 of 1

ID	Name	Type	Billings				Costs				Profit
			Billed And Collected	Billed And Not Collected	Not Billed	Total Revenue	Invoiced And Paid	Invoiced And Not Paid	Not Invoiced	Total Costs	Profit
1	job from estimate		0.00	0.00	10,081.25	10,081.25	0.00	0.00	8,065.00	8,065.00	2,016.25
1000	1000 Main Street		50,000.00	0.00	182,500.00	232,500.00	48,500.00	0.00	131,277.00	179,777.00	52,723.00
1001	505 Second Ave		0.00	0.00	230,000.00	230,000.00	0.00	0.00	171,657.00	171,657.00	58,343.00
1004	Replace Roof - 123 Main St		0.00	0.00	21,370.40	21,370.40	0.00	0.00	17,392.00	17,392.00	3,978.40
2222	200 Broadway (Model A-3)		0.00	0.00	210,000.00	210,000.00	0.00	0.00	181,402.00	181,402.00	28,598.00
			50,000.00	0.00	653,951.65	703,951.65	48,500.00	0.00	509,793.00	558,293.00	145,658.65

Logic of this report is as follows:

- **Billed And Collected.** This is the sum of all cash receipts for the job, plus the sum of all journal entries tied to an account with the Income or Receivables category.
- **Billed And Not Collected.** This is Billed minus Billed And Collected.
- **Invoiced And Paid.** This is the sum of all cash disbursements for the job, plus the sum of all journal entries tied to an account with the Inventory or Accounts Payable or Cost of Goods Sold category.
- **Invoiced And Not Paid.** This is Invoiced minus Invoiced And Paid.

Now, once you have looked at all jobs, determine if any need any more attention and then dig into those problems. Now, let's focus on specific jobs.

Reports by Job: Getting Real-Time Insight into Your Jobs

After reviewing job costs from the macro-level—comparing some or all jobs across a set of criteria, you will want to do the same on a micro-level—one job at a time.

Job Budget & Costs

This report shows job costs and compares costs to your budgets for every job you selected. It also tells you the balance of costs you need to complete the project (fig 6.5). (The example below is just the first of three pages. The final page will have totals for each column.) Here are some questions to ask when reviewing this report:

- How have my budgeted costs changed?
- What are my current costs?

FIGURE 6.5 Job budget and costs report

Vandelay Remodeling, LLC

12/6/2014 10:39:17 AM

Job Budget and Costs

Page 1 of 3

1000 - 1000 Main Street, From 12/1/2010 to 12/31/2010

| | | Job Budget | | | | Job Costs | | | | |
Job Cost	Original Estimate	Change Orders	Revised Amount	Previous Costs	Current Costs	Total Costs	Percent Complete	Over Budget	Balance to Finish
100 Preparation and Preliminaries	0.00	0.00	0.00	0.00	0.00	0.00	0.00	0.00	0.00
101 Land	27,000.00	0.00	27,000.00	27,000.00	0.00	27,000.00	100.00	0.00	0.00
103 Fees & Permits	19,000.00	0.00	19,000.00	19,000.00	0.00	19,000.00	100.00	0.00	0.00
105 Engineering & Architectural	1,000.00	0.00	1,000.00	0.00	0.00	0.00	0.00	0.00	1,000.00
107 Loan Fees	2,000.00	0.00	2,000.00	2,500.00	0.00	2,500.00	1.00	500.00	0.00
200 Excavation & Foundation	0.00	0.00	0.00	0.00	0.00	0.00	0.00	0.00	0.00
201 Excavation & Backfill	4,500.00	0.00	4,500.00	0.00	0.00	0.00	0.00	0.00	4,500.00
203 Foundation	6,875.00	0.00	6,875.00	0.00	0.00	0.00	0.00	0.00	6,875.00
205 Dampproofing	700.00	0.00	700.00	0.00	0.00	0.00	0.00	0.00	700.00
207 Structural Steel	1,735.00	0.00	1,735.00	0.00	0.00	0.00	0.00	0.00	1,735.00
300 Rough Structure	0.00	0.00	0.00	0.00	0.00	0.00	0.00	0.00	0.00
301 Framing & Siding	25,775.00	0.00	25,775.00	0.00	0.00	0.00	0.00	0.00	25,775.00
303 Trusses	2,780.00	0.00	2,780.00	0.00	0.00	0.00	0.00	0.00	2,780.00
305 Concrete Flatwork	4,247.00	0.00	4,247.00	0.00	0.00	0.00	0.00	0.00	4,247.00
307 Gutters & Downspouts	462.00	0.00	462.00	0.00	0.00	0.00	0.00	0.00	462.00
309 Plumbing	6,812.00	0.00	6,812.00	0.00	0.00	0.00	0.00	0.00	6,812.00
311 Electrical	4,291.00	0.00	4,291.00	0.00	0.00	0.00	0.00	0.00	4,291.00
313 HVAC	3,220.00	5,400.00	8,620.00	0.00	0.00	0.00	0.00	0.00	8,620.00
400 Full Enclosure	0.00	0.00	0.00	0.00	0.00	0.00	0.00	0.00	0.00
401 Roofing	2,173.00	0.00	2,173.00	0.00	0.00	0.00	0.00	0.00	2,173.00
403 Masonry	1,280.00	0.00	1,280.00	0.00	0.00	0.00	0.00	0.00	1,280.00
405 Windows & Exterior Doors	2,036.00	0.00	2,036.00	0.00	0.00	0.00	0.00	0.00	2,036.00
407 Overhead Garage Doors	578.00	0.00	578.00	0.00	0.00	0.00	0.00	0.00	578.00

- Do I have enough money in a category to complete that task?
- Where have I gone over budget?
- Why have I gone over budget (problems in estimating, vendors, etc.)?

Note: This is a key report to submit to the bank when you are processing draws!

Job-Cost Details

Used to create draws, figure 6.6 shows a detailed listing of all transactions hitting a job-cost code during a specified period of time. Here are some questions to ask when reviewing this report:

- Who am I paying this period?
- Are their insurances up to date?
- How much am I spending with each vendor?
- Does the amount I'm spending make sense?

Note: This also is a key report to submit to the bank when you are processing draws!

101

FIGURE 6.6 Job-cost details report

Job Cost	Date	Reference	Vendor	Type	Dept.	Account	Description	Debit	Credit	Balance
101		Starting Balance					Land			0.00
101	7/1/2010	1598	Drake	CD		5100	Drake Doors, LLC - To record purchase of l	27,000.00	0.00	27,000.00
101		Ending Balance					Land			27,000.00
103		Starting Balance					Fees & Permits			0.00
103	7/1/2010	1598	Drake	CD		5100	Drake Doors, LLC - To record purchase of l	19,000.00	0.00	19,000.00
103		Ending Balance					Fees & Permits			19,000.00
107		Starting Balance					Loan Fees			0.00
107	7/1/2010	1598	Drake	CD		5100	Drake Doors, LLC - To record purchase of l	2,500.00	0.00	2,500.00
107		Ending Balance					Loan Fees			2,500.00

Job-Cost Exceptions

This report prints all your job-cost exceptions in the event you want a hard copy (fig 6.7). Here are some questions to ask when reviewing this report:

- Why did I go over budget?
- Do I need to back charge another vendor?
- Do I need to issue a change order to the customer?
- Did the vendor overcharge me?
- Is it a problem in estimating?

FIGURE 6.7 Job-cost exceptions report

Vandelay Remodeling, LLC
Job Cost Exceptions
1000 - 1000 Main Street

12/6/2014 10:44:33 AM · Page 1 of 1

Job Cost	Date	Vendor	Variance Amount	Reason
107 Loan Fees	7/1/2010	Drake - Drake Doors, LLC	500.00	

Depending on your answers, you may need to document unusual variances, such as estimating errors, change orders not on estimates, sales concessions, site conditions, vandalism, and price increases. Then you can address these issues on other jobs.

Note: This may be a valuable report to submit to the bank when you are processing draws! This helps establish your credibility as a builder/contractor. Now the bank has a document as to where and why you went over budget before they need to call you for an explanation!

Job Profitability

For business owners, this is the *single most important* report you can have for a job. Why? Because, with cash flow engineering, *every* job should be profitable!

With cash flow engineering, you should also be able to generate it at any point in the job to see how much you're making and how much you're spending. With this, you can project your profitability and proactively manage your cash flow, not after the job is done. By then, it's too late.

Reports like this are the whole reason you use an integrated system: so you can see where you're going. You can see projected figures versus actual figures. Are you on the right path? You can compare how much you're billing against how much you hoped to bill. Are you on track? And you can project your profit at any stage of the job—so you spot problems that could impact your bottom line if you don't fix them. We summarize this report on both the cost side and the revenue side in figure 6.8.

FIGURE 6.8 Job profitability report

Vandelay Remodeling, LLC

12/6/2014 10:48:36 AM   Job Profitability   Page 1 of 1

1000 - 1000 Main Street, As Of 12/31/2010

ID:	1000		
Name:	1000 Main Street		
Status:	In Progress		

Billings

		Billed And Collected	50,000.00
Original Budget	225,000.00	Billed And Not Collected	0.00
Change Orders	7,500.00	Not Billed	182,500.00
Total Revenue	**232,500.00**	**Total Revenue**	**232,500.00**

Costs

		Invoiced And Paid	48,500.00
Original Budget	173,877.00	Invoiced And Not Paid	0.00
Change Orders	5,400.00	Not Invoiced	131,277.00
Total Costs	**179,277.00**	**Total Costs**	**179,777.00**

Profit	**53,223.00**	**Profit**	**52,723.00**
		Variance	**-500.00**

This report is crucial when looking at jobs. Let's go over the logic of this report:

- **Billed And Collected.** This is the sum of all cash receipts for the job.
- **Billed And Not Collected.** This lets you know what has been billed and not collected. Use this report to increase your cash-collections effort.
- **Invoiced And Paid.** This is the sum of all cash disbursements for the job.
- **Invoiced And Not Paid.** This lets you know what has been invoiced to you by vendors and not paid.

Here are some questions to ask when reviewing this report:

- Are my change orders on the sales (Billings) side equal to, if not greater than, the change orders on my cost side?
- Is every cost change order supported by a contract change order with the customer?
- Am I within budget?
- How much of what I've billed is collected and how much is still outstanding? (Make sure that if you are doing progress payments, you didn't just *bill* the customer, but you *collected* as well.)
- Is the amount left to bill still in excess of the costs-to-complete? (Too often contractors use the current job to pay for the last job. That is a surefire recipe for disaster.)
- What is my profit projection at this point in time?

These four reports above can be generated from financial reporting software like CASHFLO™ or created using spreadsheets. Before I created my software, I did this on spreadsheets in Lotus. I wrote my own macros to automate this process, but I needed a workbook for each and every house. It was very time consuming, but by tracking things at this level of detail, I saved tons of money in duplicate billings, paying for unfinished work, and making sure vendors were current on insurance.

Management Tip: When actual figures are widely different from your projections, analyze the reason and find out where the trouble spots are in your operation.

Correcting Your Trajectory

In some of the questions related to the individual reports, we gave you ways in which to correct the trajectory of the job. One more way to correct the path of the job is through change orders.

Change Orders

Once a job is set up, there is nothing more to do on the bookkeeping side than enter transactions. However, in the event you have change orders (and they can occur on the cost side, the billing side, or both), the structure is just a click away.

Remember, whenever you have a change order for your costs and you need to incur more costs to get a job done, you should also issue a change order on the billing side to bill the client for that cost. Otherwise, you eat the loss. And don't forget to add in your normal margin on the change order just like you do with the rest of the job! Actually, you can charge even more margin on change orders created during construction.

Billing and Collections

Make sure your billing is keeping pace with your costs. Billing can be done based on progress payments, draws, or percentage complete. For example (see the discussion of the production cycle approach to scheduling your receipts in Chapter 5) you can write your contract in such a way as to collect a deposit on signing of the contract and schedule various progress payments based on certain milestones. Include in these billing requests management fees to you. These management fees may be based on percentage of costs, percentage of completion or just a flat amount at each milestone. If you are a production builder, you may want to schedule draws to match your disbursement cycle. Obviously, you need to schedule your receipts to match your production cycle.

Draws

We talked about draws. I prefer to do my draws based on the standard AIA format. In this format you have cost codes going down the page vertically and for each cost code a column with the following headings:

- Original estimate
- Change orders
- Revised estimate
- Costs from previous period or draw
- Costs for the current period or draw
- Total costs
- Percent complete
- Amount over budget
- Costs to complete

Then, I prepare a list of vendors to be paid that equals the current draw amount (don't forget reimbursements and your fees). I prepare this list sorted by vendors and sorted by cost codes. I could also provide an exceptions report (answer the draw concerns before the question even comes up) and a job profitability report to show the bank and/or owner my current status.

Everything you provide that makes a draw administrators (or buyers) life easier shows professionalism on your part.

Conclusion

As you should know by now, I have a different way of looking at variable costs than accountants do. I look at them from a business owner's perspective, which I believe will make it easier for you to understand as well. More importantly, I want to help you control your variable costs to increase your company's cash flow.

Don't be misled by a quest for profit at the expense of cash flow. You need cash to pay your employees, but you also need cash to grow—because to increase volume, you need capital now to support the resources that will make the checks come in later.

Many business owners already know this, so they look to trim their costs to improve their cash flow situation. While efficiency and productivity are indeed important, they can't solve cash crunches on their own. For this, you need to focus on cash flow engineering.

Let's go back to our focus on strategy and cash flow engineering as they relate to controlling your variable costs. Our objective is to make sure our actual costs match our projected costs and the costs are reasonable for our business. This is a five step process and requires accurate, timely reports that allow you to answer relevant questions. Remember, the answers may change, but the questions seldom do. Are we on target? If not, why not?

Create Goals

To be successful in controlling variable costs we must:

_____ _____ from _____ to _____ by _____ .
     (Verb)   (Noun)   (Number) (Number)   (Date)

Create Strategies

In order to meet this goal, we will:

_____ _____ by _____, _____, & _____.
   (Verb)   (Noun)   by   (Action)   (Action) and   (Action)

As an example, maybe after reviewing your costs over several jobs you determine that you have been wasting money on each job due to reasons you have identified and can control. A goal setting statement might be:

Reduce variable costs from 80% to 75% by June 2015.

Your strategy might be:

Reduce variable costs by back charging vendors who go over budget or miss deadlines, charging clients for all change orders, and keeping jobs on schedule.

Once you've identified strategies (the "how you are going to achieve your goal"), it is time to create action plans. Action plans are a numbered list of required tasks. Each task has four components: task name, responsible party, due date, and completion status.

Once you've completed your action plan, you should evaluate the strategy's costs, effectiveness, and return on investment.

7 Controlling Fixed Costs (#7 of 7)

Overhead

Most business owners dread the first of the month. The moment the clock strikes midnight on the first day of the new month, your rent, your utilities, and your bills need to be paid. Now it's 12:01 a.m., you're already in the hole thousands of dollars, and you're going to spend the rest of the month trying to dig your way out before it's time for payroll. That's the wrong way to look at fixed costs.

The right way to look at fixed costs is much healthier for driving success: on the first of the month, you automatically *invest* thousands of dollars in your business. You're going to spend the rest of the month watching that investment pay off.

So business owners who view fixed costs as a monthly crisis have the wrong approach. Pardon the pun, but their perspective of fixed costs is broken! Fixed costs should be seen as an investment that multiplies into more time, energy, or money for the business owner.

The seventh of the 7 Key Numbers relates to controlling fixed costs. A fixed cost is easily identifiable as it typically does not change from accounting period to accounting period and will occur whether or not you have any jobs.

What exactly are fixed costs? While every business is different, there are essentially nine different business needs that incur fixed costs:

- **Salaries.** Payroll, taxes, benefits, employee training, personnel costs, and the time and energy spent performing HR-related duties
- **Property.** Rent, utilities, janitorial services, real estate taxes, parking, trash removal
- **Finance.** Bank services, loan coverage, depreciation
- **Equipment.** Computers, vehicles, tools, machines, servicing, equipment training
- **Marketing.** Advertising, web hosting, networking, business cards, design, writing
- **Professional services.** Bookkeeping, accounting, HR outsourcing, lawyer fees, paperwork, research, and other services
- **Corporate social responsibility.** Charity expenditures, volunteering, and so on
- **Insurance.** Worker's comp, liability, property
- **Other.** Supplies, admin, permits, licenses, association fees

Although you can allocate some of these costs to a job (direct costs), you will incur the cost whether you have one job or a dozen jobs. Also, note that equipment and some of the other costs may be on the *balance sheet.* But we are not looking at things from an accounting standard point but a cash flow perspective—Cash In, Cash Out!

Fixed costs fall into three major categories:

- Truly fixed costs can't be controlled such as property taxes, rent, and interest on *long-term debt.*
- Semi-variable are costs that tend to be become fixed over the short-term such as personnel costs.
- Variable costs can be controlled to some extent, such as supplies, but really aren't associated with the costs of running a job.

In cash flow engineering, your goal is to control fixed costs but in a capital-intensive environment, such as manufacturing, production, or construction, fixed costs should be relatively low as a percentage of total costs. Focusing on revenue generation and the costs associated with fulfilling the delivery of product is usually more important than just focusing on fixed costs. After all, what is the lowest that fixed costs can be? That would be zero, and if your fixed costs are zero, you are out of business.

Let's look at it another way. What is usually the largest component of fixed costs? Salaries. Whose salary is the greatest? Usually the owners (if the company is being run correctly). So what would be your motivation to decrease fixed costs when it means decreasing your salary?

What goes into the decision to generate fixed expenses?

Overhead planning should start early and permeate all phases of decision-making. You should do a complete review at least once a year. But think about this for a second. Should you only look at your overhead once a year? Of course not. In fact, overhead costs should be reflected in your budgets and reported on within your monthly income statements on a budget versus actual basis. Every month, you should see how these costs impact your business and how your business impacts your overhead. Based on the actual costs versus budgeted costs, you may need to modify your level of fixed expenses. Here are some of the criteria used to determine the level of fixed expenses:

- How decentralized should I be?
- Should I carry additional subdivisions?
- Should I lease or buy equipment?
- How far in the future does a decision at hand commit overhead expenditure?
- What are my opportunity costs?

What are the problems in controlling fixed costs?

The problem of controlling overhead differs from controlling direct costs. As a rule, this is because overhead is primarily fixed; it does not alter in dollar amount regardless of how many units you produce or homes you build. It is composed predominantly of employee compensation, marketing expenses, and general and administrative costs; it's usually a smaller percentage of sales (10% to 18%).

However, its control has a critical relationship to accurate sales forecasting and *break-even analysis* that we will discuss below. By the way, you can ask all your employees to help control variable costs, but a few top management people should control overhead.

How to Control Overhead Costs

One of the ways businesses control overhead is to budget overhead levels based upon a basic planning ratio related to various sales levels. Based on those sales levels, management should determine acceptable levels. The most important procedure involving a budget is the investigation of deviations from a plan and if necessary, subsequent corrective investigation or a revision for future periods. Integrate your budget plan with the accounting records so that variances are isolated. This is called *budget administration.*

FIGURE 7.1 Budget versus Actual report

Vandelay Remodeling, LLC

	Income Statement - Budget vs. Actual					
12/6/2014 11:41:01 AM						Page 1 of 1

Current Period from 12/1/2010 to 12/31/2010, Year to Date from 1/1/2010 to 12/31/2010, Accrual Basis

	Current Period			Year to Date		
	Actual	**Budget**	**Variance**	**Actual**	**Budget**	**Variance**
Income						
Income	63,750.00	50,000.00	13,750.00	565,219.00	600,000.00	-34,781.00
Total Income	63,750.00	50,000.00	13,750.00	565,219.00	600,000.00	-34,781.00
Cost of Goods Sold						
COGS	52,300.00	35,000.00	-17,300.00	430,773.00	420,000.00	-10,773.00
Total Cost of Goods Sold	52,300.00	35,000.00	-17,300.00	430,773.00	420,000.00	-10,773.00
Gross Margin	11,450.00	15,000.00	-3,550.00	134,446.00	180,000.00	-45,554.00
General & Admin Expenses						
Operating Expenses	22,646.24	16,205.00	-6,441.24	133,076.52	144,960.00	11,883.48
Marketing	0.00	0.00	0.00	0.00	0.00	0.00
Other Operating Expenses	0.00	0.00	0.00	0.00	0.00	0.00
Total General & Admin Expenses	22,646.24	16,205.00	-6,441.24	133,076.52	144,960.00	11,883.48
Net Operating Income (Loss)	-11,196.24	-1,205.00	-9,991.24	1,369.48	35,040.00	-33,670.52
Other Income & Expenses						
Other Operating Expenses	0.00	0.00	0.00	0.00	0.00	0.00
Total Other Income & Expenses	0.00	0.00	0.00	0.00	0.00	0.00
Net Income	-11,196.24	-1,205.00	-9,991.24	1,369.48	35,040.00	-33,670.52

In other words, regularly review budget versus actual reports. If you notice an issue, figure out what needs to be changed. Figure 7.1 shows a sample report. The variance numbers tell you immediately if you are over budget or under budget and by how much. Any time you see red, well, that's a red flag. Either your business is not operating effectively, or your costs are not appropriate for your level of sales activity.

Management Tip: When actual figures are widely different from yours, analyze the reason and find out where the trouble spots are in your operation.

Break-even Analysis

Remember, there are two major buckets for costs: our costs of production or variable costs and our fixed costs. Now it's time to relate the two and see if all our efforts will cover our costs. We do this through a tool called break-even analysis.

What is the purpose of break-even analysis?

The purpose of break-even analysis is to ensure that you have targeted a sales goal that will enable you to cover overhead. But reaching that volume is not enough.

You want to ensure that you make enough profit to justify the risk that you take and ensure an adequate salary.

For you to be profitable, you must sell a volume of your product or service that is *greater* than the *break-even point*. Finding this point requires a bit of calculation and fundamental understanding of your businesses production components.

Bottom line, at any given level of fixed costs (holding fixed costs constant within a certain range of production), the company can operate without having to increase fixed costs to a new level. The objective is to produce as many sales as possible at any given level of fixed costs. When a company jumps to a higher level of fixed costs, there is no guarantee that sales will increase enough to maintain profits.

What are the assumptions in determining your break-even point?

In determining your break-even, you need to know three things: your fixed costs, your variable costs, and your gross margin.

Again, variable costs are those costs that occur only when you have a job. These costs are a little trickier to identify in that their costs can be directly related to the product sold (i.e., the cost of producing a quarter-pound hamburger always requires quarter pound of ground beef). In the construction industry, variable costs include subcontractors, materials for a job, rental equipment, and other costs that are incurred due to a specific job. In other words, variable costs are only incurred when you produce the product itself.

Gross sales are the absolute dollar amount of sales that you record. It is calculated by taking the number of units you wish to sell (quantity) and multiplying it by the net price you get for those goods. Gross profit is the excess of net sales over the cost of goods sold (direct or variable costs). This is not your true profit because overhead has not been subtracted. This is a dollar amount (not a percentage). Gross profit percentage or margin is the gross profit divided by gross sales. This is expressed as a percentage.

What is my break-even point?

Regardless of how the break-even point is reported, all break-even analyses hinge critically on the cost of producing the product (both fixed and variable, as discussed above) and the price at which you sell the product. In short, it can be expressed formulaically as follows:

Break-even = Fixed Costs ÷ Gross profit percent

The *break-even quantity* is the total fixed costs (FC) divided by the gross profit margin (aka *contribution margin*). Think of it this way: For every dollar you make, a certain percentage is going to be used to produce and/or deliver your product. The remaining money is used to cover expenses and generate profits. More specifically, if it costs you 80 cents on the dollar to produce your product, that leaves 20 cents to cover overhead and profit. (We covered this in pricing.) This should look familiar as this is exactly the same process and formula.

Very simply, 80 cents goes out the door to pay for the product you sold, and 20 cents goes into a bucket you can use to pay for your fixed costs and take away as profit. So, if your fixed costs and profit goals total $200, you need to sell 1,000 units (each contributing $.20 to your "bucket") to break even. On the 1,001 unit, after you have paid for all your fixed costs, guess what? You can keep all 20 cents. Likewise all units sold after the necessary 1,000 until you hit the capacity your fixed costs can support.

You will note that in the 7 Key Numbers calculation, we first asked what profit level do you want to be at, your overhead costs, and finally your gross profit margin. These numbers created a sales goal. Note: this formula is a simple subtraction (Price – costs to produce the product) and division problem. Nothing fancy here.

Can you show me how this works?

Example 1: The break-even point

Let's assume that your fixed costs are $120,000 per year and your gross profit percentage is 30%; the break-even point has to be $400,000. This is determined, in any business, by taking the fixed costs, assuming they have been properly classified, and dividing by the gross profit percentage.

In our example, the $120,000 is divided by 0.30 to arrive at $400,000 of gross sales necessary to break even. This means that with a sales volume of less than $400,000, the company is operating at a loss. If the sales are in excess of $400,000, the company is profitable. If you've properly classified your fixed and variable costs, for every dollar generated over $400,000, you can put $0.30 in your pocket. This is true because your fixed costs have all been paid for by the time you hit break-even. If you have not properly classified fixed and variable costs, you will find that you have miscomputed the level at which you break even (fig 7.2).

Warning: Make sure that your base salary is included in your fixed costs; after all, you do not work for free.

What problems may I encounter in this calculation?

The greater your error in the proper classification of expenses, the less reliable the break-even point will be for making business decisions. In order to understand the

FIGURE 7.2 Break-even point with 30% gross profit percentage

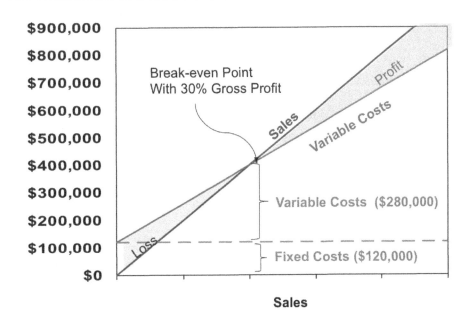

break-even point and to make decisions on how to improve profitability, you have to be sure that you have properly classified variable costs and fixed costs.

By the way, if you increase volume enough, all costs are variable. In other words, if I'm renting 5,000 square feet and I increase sales beyond a certain point, I'm going to have to rent more square footage, which means my fixed costs will have to be adjusted to a new level. Curtailing sales to remain at a current level of fixed costs can be advantageous. We'll come back to this point a little later.

What if I have various price points?

If you have departments (with different gross profit percentages) you'll have to use a composite figure to arrive at an average gross profit percentage for determining the break-even point. An example of a composite gross profit percentage may look like this:

A company has two departments, one with a 40% gross profit (from which 90% of the sales are made) and a second with a 20% gross profit (accounting for the other 10% of sales). The overall gross profit percentage is 38%, not 30% (table 7.1). This is a true composite and not the average of the different departments' gross profit percentages.

TABLE 7.1 Calculating average gross profit percentage

Gross Margin	% of Sales	Weighted
40%	90%	36%
20%	10%	2%
	100%	38%

What are the effects of decreasing my profit margin?

Example 2: Changing profit margins

In this case, you wish to expand your market share by lowering your price. When you lower your price, you will assume a decrease in your profit margin to 20% (from the original 30%). The new formula is:

$$\text{Break-even} = \$120,000 \text{ (FC)} \div .20 \text{ (profit margin)} = \$600,000$$

Notice that with a gross profit percentage of 20% and fixed costs of $120,000, it takes $600,000 per year to break even. This 10% reduction in gross profit has not only moved the break-even point out to $600,000, but each additional sales dollar after the break-even point has only 20 cents profit as opposed to 30 cents (fig 7.3)

Interestingly, some companies are under the mistaken impression that decreasing their gross profit percentage to increase sales is a great idea. But looking at that

FIGURE 7.3 Break-even point with 20% gross profit percentage

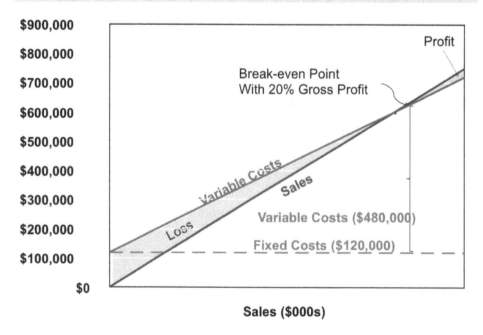

Sales ($000s)

critically, you can clearly see that decreasing gross profit percentage to increase sales or increase market may be a bad idea because the action increases your break-even point *and* decreases the net profit the company earns for each sale over and above the break-even point.

Lowering prices can help a company increase market share in the short run. However, it can also create some significant financial hurdles. In this case, you now have to sell $600,000 worth of product just to break even, which means a 50% increase in sales (from $400,000 to $600,000) without making a dime more than you would have. Do you really want to work harder for nothing? The point to be made in this break-even comparison is that lowering prices may increase market share but at the cost of far more financial risk.

Table 7.2 shows you how much sales need to increase in order for you to maintain the same gross profit in absolute dollars. For instance, if your gross margin is 20% (along the top row of the table) and you decrease prices by 10% (down the left side of the table), you would need to increase your gross sales by 100% (in the middle of the table) in order to make the same margin. In other words, you are doing twice the work for the same amount of money.

TABLE 7.2 Gross profit margin at various prices

		Your Gross Profit Margin is						
		10%	15%	20%	25%	30%	40%	50%
Percentage you lower your prices	2%	25	15	11	9	7	5	4
	4%	67	36	25	19	15	11	9
	6%	150	67	47	36	25	18	14
	8%	400	114	67	47	36	25	19
	10%		200	100	67	50	33	25
	12%		400	150	92	67	43	32
	14%		1400	233	127	88	54	39
	16%			400	178	114	67	47
	18%			900	257	150	82	56
	20%				400	200	100	67
	25%					500	167	100
	30%						300	150

So what can be done?

Perhaps the best strategy is to cut costs. Instead of decreasing profit by lowering price, you might want to consider cutting costs, keeping your price constant, and reaping the benefits of a greater gross profit percentage.

If it's necessary to lower prices to create more business, you should investigate all channels to buy at lower prices. Buying at lower prices will allow you to have competitive pricing and still maintain a good gross profit margin.

For example, a carpet store buys a given carpet at $6.00 per yard and retails it for $9.00. Perhaps a trip to the factory would allow for a reduced price on a volume purchase of first-rate goods, which are being discontinued. If carpet that normally costs $6.00 can be purchased for $4.00, the merchant might sell it at $7.00. Be careful of the pitfalls with absolute dollars and percentages. In our example, you still make $3.00 per yard on sales, but your gross profit percentage has increased (table 7.3).

TABLE 7.3 Effect of changing costs and prices on gross profit percentage

	Before	After
Price	$9.00	$7.00
Cost	$6.00	$4.00
Gross Margin	$3.00	$3.00
GM %	33%	43%

The competition from the big chains has made it very difficult for the small shop to compete. One of your defenses to stay competitive with your sales price and still make a decent gross profit would be to become a member of a buying association or investigate quantity buying on your own.

How do I set a sales goal that includes a desired level of profit?

Example 3: Including profit in the break-even calculation

The break-even formula can also be adjusted to include a desired level of profit, debt reduction, and other balance sheet expenditures in order to estimate cash flow break-even. Assume that $30,000 is the desired net profit. Thus:

$$\$120,000 \text{ (FC)} + \$30,000 \text{ (profit)} = \$150,000$$

Then, $150,000 would be divided by 30%. The new break-even point would be $500,000 (the original starting point was $400,000). Thus by increasing your sales by $100,000, you generated the $30,000 profit you desire. How can that be? Well, $400,000 was the volume you needed to break even. Once you get there, each additional unit you sell gives you 30 cents in profit with no associated costs. Thus, if you increase sales by $100,000 and keep 30% of it, you have $30,000. Again, this assumes that you have the capacity to generate that much volume with no additional fixed costs.

How can I use the break-even point to make other decisions?

Example 4: Assessing the effect of sales compensation on break-even
Let's start from example 3, including profit in the break-even calculation.

Case 1: Hire a salesperson based on commission only.
Suppose you want to target a $30,000 profit and use a target of 5% of sales for marketing. This means your variable cost increases by 5% and your margin decreases by 5%. Then your formula would be:

$$Q = \frac{\$120,000 \text{ (FC)} + \$30,000 \text{ (profit)}}{30\% \text{ (margin)} - 5\%}$$

In this case, your break-even point would be:

$$\frac{\$150,000}{.25} = \$600,000$$

This would be $150,000 divided by .25% or the new break-even point would be $600,000. Thus, sales would have to increase by $100,000 to cover the sales commissions of 5%.

Case 2: Hire a salesperson based on salary only.
Suppose you want to pay a salesperson a flat fee of $30,000 per year instead of commission. Again your formula would be:

$$\frac{\$120,000 \text{ (FC)} +\$30,000 \text{ (employee)} +\$30,000 \text{ (profit)}}{.30 \text{ (profit margin)}} = \frac{\$180,000}{.30} = \$600,000$$

This would be $180,000 divided by 30% so the new break-even point would be $600,000. Now, sales would have to increase by $100,000 to generate the $30,000 profit.

If you wanted to calculate the impact of a "base plus commission" structure, you just adjust both the numerator (add in the base to the fixed costs) and denominator (subtracting the commission rate from your margin) and do the same calculation.

Can I calculate my break-even point in units?

Suppose you only have one product and you need to know your break-even point in units. In this case, instead of dividing by a profit margin (which is a percentage), you will divide by the contribution margin. Contribution margin is the price minus the variable cost per unit. It is expressed in dollars. It is called contribution, as it states how much money is left to cover overhead and profit after you sell the unit. For instance, suppose that you sell a product at a $100 and your cost is $70 per unit. Your contribution margin is $30 (your profit margin is 30%). Then your formula would be:

$$\frac{\$120,000 \ (FC) + \$30,000 \ (profit)}{\$30 \ (the \ dollar \ contribution \ margin)}$$

This would be $150,000 divided by $30 or the new break-even point would be 5,000 units. If you multiply the 5,000 by the price of $100 per unit, you would need sales of $500,000. This is the same answer as in example 3.

What is a relevant range?

In the first example, the company had fixed costs of $120,000 and a gross profit percentage of 30%, resulting in a break-even point of $400,000. Imagine they can still produce more than that given the same level of fixed costs. Let's say the company can operate up to $500,000 in sales without having to increase fixed costs. But, let's assume that you now have to spend an additional $60,000 to support growth beyond this level. All things being equal (i.e., profit margins stay the same), what would be your new break-even point? Your fixed costs increased to $180,000 and revenue would have to increase to $600,000 just to break even again.

$$\frac{\$180,000 \ (FC)}{.30 \ (profit \ margin)} = \$600,000$$

The company had to increase sales by 50% (from $400,000 to $600,000) to cover a $60,000 increase in fixed costs.

Figure 7.4 depicts this example. The "steps" moving up to the right show the current level of fixed costs ($120,000) in the center and a higher level of fixed costs (at $180,000). It also shows the *relevant ranges* for each level. At the $120,000 of fixed costs, you break even at $400,000 but can produce up to $500,000 of sales (point B on the graph). At this point, you can choose to invest another $60,000 to jump up to point C, which is a loss. As sales increase, you can eventually get to point D, which is the highest level of production with this level of fixed overhead.

As an alternative, as the sales volume starts pushing the $500,000 level, the company should look at controlling growth as opposed to expanding to some larger facility with the hope that the sales will continue to grow. The closer the company

FIGURE 7.4 Relevant ranges

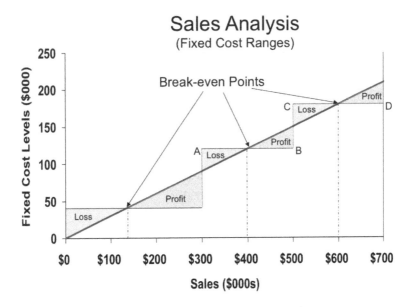

(in this example) is to point B, the more profitable it has become. It is in the interest of any company to produce as many sales as possible at a given level of fixed costs. However, with the current capacity of the plant, it can't exceed this level without a breakdown in the company (overtime, machine breakage, down time, etc.).

Controlling Growth

As an alternative to growing too fast and outstripping your assets, perhaps the business owner should look at controlling sales with by increasing the gross profit percentage (by increasing your price). Not only will this limit the growth in sales, but it increases the profits in the resulting sales!

Let that sink in. How often do you hear someone suggest you *deliberately lower* demand for your products or services? I hope you understand now why that may make sense for your business, even if it violates common sense? The common-sense approach often does not consider the far-reaching impacts on all the areas of your business. The 7 Key Numbers look at everything and help you pinpoint the best strategies to increase your company's cash flow.

Suppose that this company was running a 30% gross profit and sitting right at point B, with a lot of pressure on it to expand the size of its operations. By increasing the gross profit percentage by two points, two things happen. First, the company lowers the break-even point down to $375,000 from $400,000.

$$\frac{\$120,000 \ (FC)}{.32 \ (\text{profit margin})} = \$375,000$$

In addition to dropping the break-even point, they have increased the overall profit on $500,000 of sales, from $30,000 to $40,000 net (table 7.4).

TABLE 7.4 The effect of changing profit margin on profit

	Before	After
Sales	500,000	500,000
Profit margin %	30%	32%
Gross profit	150,000	160,000
Fixed costs	120,000	120,000
Profit	30,000	40,000

If you are an operation with limited financial backing, there's a lot to be said for controlling the growth of the company. If you can increase net profit by increasing gross profit percentage and, in turn, control growth to keep from having to expand fixed costs, you may have won on two fronts. First, you increased profitability, and second, you eliminated the risk that the increased fixed costs may have put you in financial jeopardy.

When a company jumps to a higher level of fixed costs, there is nothing that says the sales will increase enough to put the company back into the profitability status it now has. Before you expand your business, analyze the benefits of staying small. Maximize your net profits at your current level.

Goal Setting and Strategy

Take the time to create strategies to help you control your fixed costs. Remember, your objective may not be just to lower overhead costs but possibly to increase overhead costs (to compensate you and your employees, to invest in marketing and sales, and/or invest in company growth).

Focus on Strategy

To be successful in controlling overhead, you must:

_____ _____ from _____ to _____ by _____.
    (Verb)   (Noun)   (Number) (Number)   (Date)

In order to meet this goal, you will:

_____ _____ by _____, _____, & _____.
   (Verb)   (Noun)   by   (Action)   (Action)   and   (Action)

As an example, maybe after performing your break-even analysis, you find that you must cut costs. One goal setting statement might be:

Reduce monthly fixed costs from $10,000 to $8,000 by June 2015.

Your strategy might be:

Reduce fixed costs by outsourcing bookkeeping, streamlining inter-department communication, and adapting time-tracking systems.

Once you've identified strategies (the "how you are going to achieve your goal"), it is time to create action plans. Action plans are a numbered list of required tasks. Each task has four components: task name, responsible party, due date, and completion status.

Once you've completed your action plan, you should evaluate the strategy's costs, effectiveness, and return on investment.

Conclusion

Let's talk about controlling costs in general (both fixed and variable). You should always control costs but control costs as it relates to a certain volume of revenue. How often have you walked into a restaurant to find that they are cutting costs? It might have taken a couple of minutes to order and get your food, but now they are understaffed (because the bean counters are focused on cutting costs); it is a painful experience. Meanwhile, the business breeds unhappy customers who don't come back. Revenue drops, and the bean counters start cutting more staff. But the bean counters forget that zero is the lowest costs can go. And at zero, you are out of business (you can't even pay yourself). Control costs if there is inefficiency, otherwise keep your business customer centric.

As a builder and business owner, your three most important business resources are time, money, and energy. This broad view is important. Most business owners fixate on conserving money and doing so quickly exhausts their time and energy. Let's define these resources from a business owner's perspective:

- **Time.** This refers to your time only. It does not include your employees' time because you pay for their time with another of your resources, money.
- **Energy.** This is your concentration, frustration, mental effort, and emotional engagement. The energy you devote to your business cannot be calculated in dollars and cents, but you can measure it on a relative scale of 1 to 10.
- **Money.** This is both labor and non-labor costs. Labor costs vary depending upon the employee, and non-labor costs, such as materials and supplies, vary according to the market.

One of the keys to running a successful business is managing your outflow of all three resources.

Know Your Costs So You Can Cut Them

As we've discussed, your business has two kinds of costs: fixed and variable. Fixed costs, which generally don't change over a defined time period, include items such as salaries and office rent.

Variable costs are incurred during the production of a product. They include labor, raw materials, equipment rentals, and other necessary costs when building a home.

To manage your costs (not just money, but time and energy as well) you need to identify all your costs and then reduce them. Let's talk about doing this for variable costs. This happens in two steps:

- Inventory your entire production process to see where your resources (time, energy, and money) are being spent.
- Develop and execute strategies to balance the production activities that are consuming too many of your resources.

List each activity in your production cycle. This includes everything that's involved in selling and building a new home, which clearly begins long before the foundation is dug. In fact, your complete production cycle can likely be grouped into six activity hubs:

- Acquiring the lead
- Closing the lead
- Completing the sale
- Construction
- Punch list and completion
- Warranty and follow-up

Once you've listed all the activities that comprise each activity hub, you should calculate the time, money, and energy each one requires. Then look through the list to see which activities cost an inordinate amount of your time, money, or energy.

Then, determine how you can balance your resource usage. For example, if something is very time-intensive, can you substitute money instead of time? (That means hiring someone to do it for you, for example.) Or if something is very energy intensive and it wipes you out for the rest of the day, is there a way you can spread the effort over time to make it less exhausting?

8

Financial Management

As a CPA, I would be remiss if I didn't spend some time on financial management, which is more than looking at your books and financial statements. I tend to be a maverick in this area, as I believe that financial statements should confirm what you *should* already know. After all, if you're monitoring your 7 Key Numbers on a daily basis, then there should be no surprises.

Financial statements are a lagging indicator not a current indicator. They are historical records, not real-time snapshots of your company. As a business owner, you also need to keep track of leading indicators and non-financial indicators. You need to know how many leads you are generating, how well you are converting the leads to customers, and how you are doing in terms of customer retention and referrals. You also need to measure pricing and gross profit margins on all your products and number of transactions per customer. Although these numbers are so vitally important to a business owner, these numbers don't usually come from your accounting system. You need these numbers whether you create a spreadsheet yourself or invest in financial software.

There is a problem with accounting systems—they only record historical events (what has already happened) and the reports generated from historical data fail in many ways to give managers the information that they need for current control. Think about it. The financial statements are usually monthly, quarterly, or annual. That means at least a month has passed since some of the data was generated.

Ordinary accounting systems may not produce the data managers need to validate pricing decisions. For example, overhead and periodic expense may be incurred without regard to units produced. Accounting systems may not show the builder where he stands currently and on a timely basis.

Having said that, do not disregard or discount financial statements. Indeed, understanding financial statements is critical to the success of a business. Think of it this way: bookkeeping records the day-to-day transactions involved in running the business. In other words, they keep track of every management decision that has a financial impact. The transactions are then summarized into financial statements. Used to their full extent, they are tools necessary to propel the company forward and increase the value of the company.

Financial statements are absolutely important in reporting to stakeholders (absentee owners, the board of directors, etc.), banks, and other third parties. As I said in Chapter 1, a frequent statement I hear from business brokers is that they have trouble valuing the business as the financial statements weren't used to position the company for sale. Most bankers complain that the story the financial statements tell doesn't allow them to make meaningful capital injections into the business. So a critical question when reviewing your financial statements is, "What story are they telling?"

Financial Statements

Understanding financial statements is critical to running a successful business. On a simple level, financial statements provide information about how your business is working on a daily basis. Once you fully understand how to read and use financial statements, they are the tools needed to understand and analyze long-term trends and to plan for long-term growth and profit.

To understand how financial statements work, it is necessary to view them within the larger context of financial management, which is detailed in the sections that follow.

The 5 C's Process of Financial Management

We covered the 5 C's process in Chapter 1 and Chapter 6. Now let's focus on using the 5 C's process on your accounting and financial management:

1. **Create** your benchmarks
2. **Collect** meaningful information
3. **Compile** your data
4. **Compare** your results
5. **Correct** your trajectory

Financial statements fall within the Compile step. As my accountant friends like to point out, this puts them smack dab at the center of financial management. Let's use the 5 C's to analyze our financial statements.

Step 1—Create

Create your expectations through a business plan and related budgets that support it. A business plan is based on historical data, the economic environment, demographics, and customer research. Based on your business plan and the data from which it is created, you can realistically project sales levels for a given time period. This sales projection, in turn, drives the budget(s) for the costs associated with your business.

Successful companies distinguish themselves from less successful companies with their ability to create accurate budget forecasts that account for fluctuations in fixed- and variable-expense costs. In general, the following features and benefits characterize an accurate budget forecast:

- It requires only basic financial data taken from your company's historical records or through comparisons to industry statistics.
- It enables you to present vital information graphically to enhance understanding of how a company will perform.
- It helps you to see monthly costs and identify potential areas of savings.
- It helps you to identify potential cash needs.
- It helps in the process of making decisions on timing and the use of funds.
- It provides critical information for management in short-term expected profitability.
- It allows a company to develop targeted strategies to address shortfalls in cash flow.

While financial statements are used to record history for a company, budgets are used to show what the future should look like for that company. Figure 8.1 is a sample of a consolidated budget for 2010. Consider presenting the budget graphically as well which can enhance and simplify understanding.

FIGURE 8.1 Sample budget

Vandelay Remodeling, LLC
Budget for 2010
Prepared by: I.M. Counting

	Jan	Feb	Mar		Nov	Dec	Total
Sales	50,000	45,000	55,000	::	45,000	43,000	600,000
Cost of Goods Sold	35,000	31,500	38,500	::	31,500	30,100	420,000
	-------	-------	-------	::	-------	-------	-------
Gross Margin	15,000	13,500	16,500	::	13,500	12,900	180,000
				::			
Salaries & Wages	1,750	1,750	1,750	::	1,750	1,750	21,000
Salaries & Wages - Officers	5,292	5,292	5,292	::	5,292	5,292	63,500
Employer Taxes	750	750	750	::	750	750	9,000
Employee Benefits	333	333	333	::	333	333	4,000
Advertising	417	417	417	::	417	417	5,000
Auto Expenses	125	125	125	::	125	125	1,500
Bad Debts	42	42	42	::	42	42	500
Bank Fees	125	125	125	::	125	125	1,500
Computer & Internet Expenses	125	125	125	::	125	125	1,500
Depreciation	375	375	375	::	375	375	4,500
Insurance	375	375	375	::	375	375	4,500
Interest	125	125	125	::	125	125	1,500
Legal & Professional	625	625	625	::	625	625	7,500
Meals & Entertainment	158	158	158	::	158	158	1,900
Office & Shop Expenses	250	250	250	::	250	250	3,000
Permits & Fees	83	83	83	::	83	83	1,000
Phone	200	200	200	::	200	200	2,400
Postage & Freight	100	100	100	::	100	100	1,200
Printing	125	125	125	::	125	125	1,500
Rent	625	625	625	::	625	625	7,500
Repairs	83	83	83	::	83	83	1,000
Other Operating Expenses				::			
	-------	-------	-------	::	-------	-------	-------
Total Operaing Expenses	12,083	12,083	12,083	::	12,083	12,083	145,000
	-------	-------	-------	::	-------	-------	-------
Net Operating Income (Before Taxes)	2,917	1,417	4,417	::	1,417	817	35,000

Step 2—Collect

Collect the financial and non-financial data needed to track the progress of your business. Financial data includes information, such as estimates, job costs, exception reports, and accounting records. Non-financial data includes information, such as the number of sales, sales per salesperson, revenue per employee, traffic counts, and customer profiles.

What is the difference between cash flow and profit?

An axiom I use in analyzing businesses is this: A business can survive without profit, but it cannot survive one day without cash.

Let's analyze this! Financially, only two things are really happening: Cash comes in and cash goes out. If there is positive cash flow (more cash coming in than going out on a consistent basis) then money is available to do a variety of other things.

You must monitor your cash at every point because the only time that you can really take money out of your business without killing it is when the money is coming in faster than it is going out.

Cash comes in from a variety of sources: operations (sales of your products or services), new debt and capital (owner) infusions of cash. It goes out to pay for operations, purchase assets (inventory, fund receivables, pay back debt, buy assets or pay dividends (distributions, owner withdrawals). But, if you look at figure 8.2, you will see a vertical dash line which delineates the difference between "owner think" and "accountants think".

FIGURE 8.2 Cash inflows and outflows

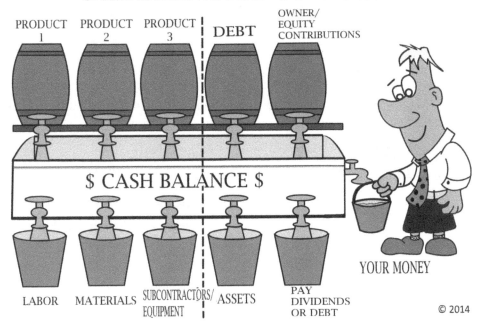

You see, the reason it is so hard to manage to your financial statements is that most owners think in terms of money coming in and money going out of their business.

On the left of the dash line is operational items—things that appear on your income statement. Sales (both cash and those accrued—sales without cash) and expenses related to the production of that income. Things on the right of the dashed line normally show up on the balance sheet. That includes cash expended for purchases of inventory (construction in process), tangible and intangible assets, cash used to pay back debt and *equity*. It also includes cash received from debt and equity. So, this illustrates that cash in and cash out show up *both* on the balance sheet and income statement. Is it any wonder that so many business owners have trouble understanding their financial statements? It doesn't show if you are building wealth or not! We'll talk more about financial statements below as they do serve a purpose in understanding your business.

The balance sheet looks at where the money that funds the organization is coming from (primarily debt and equity) and how it is being spent (asset purchases, material purchases, work in process, fixed assets, dividends, owners withdrawals, and payments on debt, etc.). These are the items on the right side of the dotted line. Sometimes one has to question the structure of financial statements. I think a better reflection would be a summary of cash flow the way an owner thinks.

Step 3—Compile

There are four basic reports included in financial statements:

- **Balance sheet.** Shows what a company has, what it owes, and what is left for the owner(s).
- **Income satement.** Tells how much a company is making, its profitability.
- *Cash flow statement.* Tells where money comes from and where it goes.
- **Trial balance.** Lists all the accounts and their balances. The sum of the debits and credits must equal zero. Then you are in "balance."

Where does the information in my financial statements come from?

Bookkeeping is the part of accounting that records the flow of transactions into and out of a business. The bookkeeping process can be summarized as follows:

- Transactions
- Journals
- Ledger
- Financial statements

Simply explained, in every business, management creates various types of transactions, which are summarized in different journals and then posted in the general ledger. The information in the general ledger, in turn, is compiled into the three basic types of financial statements. The next sections explain each part of the bookkeeping process prior to compilation into financial statements.

1. Transactions

Transactions are created from daily operations and from managerial decisions. *Operating transactions* include everyday activities such as sales and purchases. Other transactions include the acquisition of capital assets or the borrowing of money. Bookkeeping identifies and classifies transactions to determine their effects on the balances of a firm's assets, *liabilities*, or equity.

2. Journals

Journals are the books into which transactions are chronologically entered, either on a daily or weekly basis. Journals are the source documents for the general ledger. Each month, the new journal data is added to the existing data in the general ledger. Most accounting systems use five standard journals:

- The *purchase* journal records bills as they are received from your suppliers.
- The *cash disbursements* journal records each transaction that involves check writing or cash distribution.
- The *sales* journal records all sales made on account to customers.
- The *cash receipts* journal records each receipt of cash and bank deposit transaction.
- The *general* journal records all transactions that do not fit in the other journals.

Each journal records approximately ten pieces of data for each transaction:

- Source journal abbreviation
- Account number
- Class (if using depts.)
- Vendor/customer
- Description of the transaction
- Reference number (e.g., invoice number, P.O. number, customer number)
- Reference date
- Dollar amount of the transaction
- Job number
- Job-cost account

3. General ledger

The general ledger is the master record into which all transactions are compiled. It maintains the balances of all the accounts, including assets, liabilities, equity, income, and expenses. While journals are organized chronologically, the general ledger is organized by account number, providing a business with two views of the information—one of monthly records and totals and one of the overall annual picture by category. In addition, the general ledger contains the following information:

- The account number of every account in the chart of accounts
- The account title
- Beginning balances for the year
- Ending balances for the year
- Total postings by month
- Budgets for each account

4. Financial Statements

The information is now compiled from the general ledger into the four basic financial statements, which are prepared according to generally accepted accounting principles, (GAAP). Generally accepted accounting principles are the rules, conventions, practices, and procedures that are the foundation of financial accounting. Most certified accounting professionals use these principles to compile, review, or audit financial reports. More importantly, using GAAP enables different sizes and types of business to account for their finances and report them in a standardized format that allows a third party, such as a bank, to easily see and understand a company's financial position.

How do I interpret the balance sheet?

A balance sheet is often described as a snapshot of a company's financial status at a given moment in time—typically at the end of a financial period (though they can also be monthly, quarterly, or on demand). A balance sheet is created from three types of information:

- **Assets**
- **Liabilities**
- **Equity**

Mathematically, the balance sheet is assets equals liabilities plus equity. Assets are usually on the left side of a balance sheet. Liabilities and equity are usually on the right side. The two sides must have the same value—that's why it is called a balance sheet.

Let's look at the balance sheet in more detail. The asset side of the balance shows the resources of the organization.

- **Assets.** Assets are economic resources expected to produce economic benefits for their owner. They can be buildings, machinery, patents, copyrights, or even money owed to the firm by customers. Assets fall within two categories:
  - » Current. Assets that will be transformed into cash or used within one year (or the normal operating cycle if more than one year). Typical examples include cash, marketable securities, accounts receivable, inventories, and pre-paid expenses.
  - » Non-current. Assets that will not be consumed within one year, or the normal operating cycle. Typical non-current (also called long-term) assets include tangible items, such as property, the plant, and equipment and intangible items, such as patents, copyrights, and goodwill.

  The rationale for having two types of assets (i.e., current and non-current) is to highlight liquidity and thus assist in predicting cash flow.

- **Liabilities.** Liabilities are obligations a company owes to outside parties. They represent the rights of others to money or services from the company. Typical examples are bank loans and debts to suppliers or employees. Like assets, liabilities are either current or non-current:
  - » Current. Claims against a company that will be satisfied within a year (or the normal operating cycle). Typical examples include accounts payable, wages payable, accrued expenses, taxes payable, and the current portion of notes payable.
  - » Non-current. Liabilities that are outstanding for more than a year or the normal operating cycle. Typical non-current liabilities include mortgages, bonds payable, and long-term notes. Keep in mind that non-current liabilities can be current at the same time if part of the liability must be satisfied within the current year or normal operating cycle.

- **Equity.** The value of a business to its owners after all obligations have been met. This *net worth* (i.e., the difference between what it owns and what it owes) belongs to the owners, or is owner-invested capital. There are two broad classes of equity.
  - » Capital contributions. Funds from the owners of the company
  - » Retained earnings. Any profits that are reinvested into the company

Figure 8.3 shows a typical balance sheet. It illustrates how the three basic areas balance, as well as the smaller categories into which the areas are broken down. More importantly, a balance sheet can be used to compare a company's financial health to both industry-wide and internal benchmarks.

FIGURE 8.3 Typical balance sheet

Vandelay Remodeling, LLC

Balance Sheet - Detail
As of 12/31/2010

Assets		Liabilities & Members' Equity	
Current Assets		**Liabilities**	
1005 - Cash Account	1,759.85	**Current Liabilities**	
Receivables	51,250.00	Deposits & Escrows	0.00
Deposits	0.00	Accounts Payable	8,799.85
Inventory	35,150.00	Taxes Payable	0.00
Prepaid Expenses	0.00	Accrued Expenses	0.00
Total Current Assets	88,159.85	Current Portion of Long Term	0.00
		Total Current Liabilities	8,799.85
Investments			
Investments	0.00	**Long Term Liabilities**	
Total Investments	0.00	Long Term Debt	32,000.00
		Mortgages Payable	0.00
Fixed Assets		**Total Long Term Liabilities**	32,000.00
Fixed Assets	45,000.00	**Total Liabilities**	40,799.85
Accumulated Depreciation	-9,000.00		
Total Fixed Assets	36,000.00	**Member's Equity**	
		3100 - Members Capital - 1	66,650.00
Other Assets		Retained Earnings	15,340.52
Other Assets	0.00	Current Year Earnings	1,369.48
Total Other Assets	0.00	**Total Member's Equity**	83,360.00
Total Assets	124,159.85	**Total Liabilities & Member's**	124,159.85

Unaudited - For Management Purposes Only

Questions to ask when interpreting a balance sheet

To interpret a balance sheet, the reader must ask the following questions:

- **Does the company have the proper level of fixed assets?** Fixed assets should not be so excessive so as to reduce a company's ability to continue operating.
- **Does the company have sufficient working capital to handle sales volume?**
- **Is the company solvent?** There should be enough assets to adequately cover all debt.
- **Can the company pay its bills?** There should be enough cash to cover all current expenses.
- **Is the company building wealth?** If the equity on the current balance sheet is compared to the equity on previous balance sheets, there should be an overall increase, thereby showing growth in wealth.

How do I interpret the income statement?

An income statement, sometimes called a *profit and loss (P & L) statement,* shows how much money a company is making or losing over a given time period. More specifically, it summarizes the transactions that occur over the time period in terms of revenues and expenses. Revenues are inflows of resources like cash and other assets attributed to goods or services provided; and expenses are the outflows of resources incurred in profit-making activities.

An income statement, like a balance sheet, can be compared to industry-wide averages for similar data and serves multiple purposes:

- It indicates whether a company is making a profit.
- It can be used to help determine tax liability.
- It can be used to measure and control costs by looking at costs as a percentage of sales.
- It serves as a guide to potential lenders and/or investors by providing an indication of past performance, which is often seen as an indicator of future performance.

Despite its utility, an income statement alone cannot tell a reader whether a company is generally building or destroying wealth. To provide a complete financial picture of a company, an income statement must be viewed together with a balance sheet and a cash flow statement.

An income statement is organized in "steps" that highlight key financial points for a company. In figure 8.4 you can see how each step proceeds in order to a distinct piece of financial data.

FIGURE 8.4 The steps of an income statement

Net Sales (gross revenue)		
Cost of Goods Sold (COGS)		
Net Sales – COGS = Gross Margin		
Operating Expenses		
Gross Margin – Operating Expenses = Operating Profit		
Non-Operating Income		
Non-Operating Expense		
Operating Profit +/– Non-operating Income/Expense = Net income		

To read and understand an income statement, it is first necessary to understand the basic terminology:

- **Net Sales.** Gross sales minus sales returns, sales allowances, and sales discounts.
- **Cost of goods sold (COGS).** This is the net cost of bringing goods to market during the period covered by the statement. The accounting definition is more precise than simply tracking how much it costs to make each unit. It also tracks the flow of inventory and inventory-related costs in and out of a business. The reason is simple. This month, you may sell some products you actually produced last month. And you may make some products this month that you won't sell until next month.

COGS = Beginning Inventory + Cost of Goods Produced/Purchased –
Ending Inventory

- **Gross margin** (also gross income or gross profit). The amount available to pay marketing expenses and overhead.

Gross Margin = Gross Revenues – COGS

- **Operating expenses.** All expenses related to the sale of merchandise or services (selling expenses) plus all other costs related to operating the business (general and administrative expenses, marketing, finance, etc.).
- **Net income/net loss.** Generated when revenues exceed expenses, or conversely, when expenses exceed revenues.
- **Non-operating income/non-operating expenses.** The results of activities other than those for which the business was originally organized such as interest income or rent. They can either be included on an income statement separately, or as part of the other revenue and expenses.
- **Extraordinary gains/losses.** Significant or material gains or losses resulting from events that are *both* unusual in nature and infrequent in occurrence. Examples include casualty losses, debt, and capital restructuring. Extraordinary gains and losses are shown net of tax effects.
- **Non-recurring items.** Material gains or losses resulting from events that are *either* unusual in nature or infrequent in occurrence, such as the sale of property or other operating assets.

Figure 8.5 shows a sample income statement. At the end of each year, a business's income and expense accounts are closed out and the profit is transferred to the equity section of the balance sheet. More specifically, the profit appears in a category or account called *retained earnings*. Retained earnings indicate the cumulative, undistributed profit built up in a business.

FIGURE 8.5 Sample income statement

Vandelay Remodeling, LLC
Income Statement - Detail
Current Period from 12/1/2010 to 12/31/2010, Year to Date from 1/1/2010 to 12/31/2010

	Current Period		Year to Date	
Income				
4100 - Sales	63,750.00	100.00%	565,219.00	100.00%
Total Income	63,750.00	100.00%	565,219.00	100.00%
Cost of Goods Sold				
5100 - Cost of Goods Sold	43,800.00	68.71%	422,273.00	74.71%
5101 - Supplies	8,500.00	13.33%	8,500.00	1.50%
Total Cost of Goods Sold	52,300.00	82.04%	430,773.00	76.21%
Gross Margin	11,450.00	17.96%	134,446.00	23.79%
General & Admin Expenses				
6010 - Salaries &Wages	0.00	0.00%	26,250.00	4.64%
6020 - Salaries & Wages - Officers	0.00	0.00%	55,000.00	9.73%
6040 - Employer Taxes	0.00	0.00%	8,635.00	1.53%
6050 - Employee Benefits	0.00	0.00%	3,978.00	0.70%
6110 - Advertising	0.00	0.00%	2,500.00	0.44%
6150 - Auto Expenses	0.00	0.00%	976.77	0.17%
6160 - Bad Debts	0.00	0.00%	348.75	0.06%
6170 - Bank Fees	625.00	0.98%	625.00	0.11%
6200 - Computer & Internet Expenses	0.00	0.00%	1,603.00	0.28%
6230 - Depreciation	4,500.00	7.06%	4,500.00	0.80%
6280 - Insurance	0.00	0.00%	3,000.00	0.53%
6320 - Interest	0.00	0.00%	2,500.00	0.44%
6330 - Legal & Professional	6,500.00	10.20%	6,500.00	1.15%
6360 - Meals & Entertainment	1,700.00	2.67%	1,700.00	0.30%
6370 - Office & Shop Expenses	0.00	0.00%	1,299.85	0.23%
6380 - Permits & Fees	0.00	0.00%	295.00	0.05%
6390 - Phone	0.00	0.00%	2,567.32	0.45%
6400 - Postage & Freight	953.75	1.50%	953.75	0.17%
6410 - Printing	0.00	0.00%	1,476.59	0.26%
6420 - Rent	7,500.00	11.76%	7,500.00	1.33%
6430 - Repairs	867.49	1.36%	867.49	0.15%
Marketing	0.00	0.00%	0.00	0.00%
Other Operating Expenses	0.00	0.00%	0.00	0.00%
Total General & Admin Expenses	22,646.24	35.52%	133,076.52	23.54%
Net Operating Income (Loss)	-11,196.24	-17.56%	1,369.48	0.24%
Non-Operating Income & Expenses				
Other Operating Expenses	0.00	0.00%	0.00	0.00%
Total Non-Operating Income & Expenses	0.00	0.00%	0.00	0.00%
Net Income	-11,196.24	-17.56%	1,369.48	0.24%

Unaudited - For Management Purposes Only

How do I interpret the cash flow statement?

The cash flow statement, also known as a statement of change in financial position, provides information on a company's financial policies and strategies by disclosing two categories of information:

- **Sources of funds.** including profits from operations, long-term borrowing, and issuance of capital stock proceeds through the sale of long-term assets
- **Uses of funds.** including outlays for purchases of fixed assets or intangibles, investments in stock, payments of cash dividends, and repayment of long-term debt

Note: The term fund can mean cash, cash and near cash, or working capital.

By definition, a cash flow statement is essentially a reformulated balance sheet and income statement combination supplemented with information from the notes to the financial statements. A cash flow statement documents changes either in cash and cash equivalents or in working capital by examining changes in balance sheet accounts. Since a balance sheet must balance, so too must a cash flow statement. The net source must equal the difference in cash.

The Concept of Cash Flow From an Accountant's Point of View

Just by the title of this section you can see my bias. I think this statement is extremely hard to read and interpret. Before detailing the methodology and structure of a cash flow statement, an introduction to the concept of cash flow itself is necessary. From an accounting perspective, cash comes from three components:

- **Operating activities.** Funds generated or used internally as part of normal business activities
- **Investing activities.** Funds generated or used that impact the non-current assets on the balance sheet, such as plant and equipment and investment activities
- **Financing activities.** Externally generated funds that impact long-term debt, such as the issuance or redemption of bonds or loans and/or equity (i.e., the issuance or redemption of stock), as reflected on the balance sheet

To understand the nature of cash flow, consider the fact that a business can survive without profit, but not without cash. This is true because profit is only one area of a larger financial picture. Cash is not generated or spent solely through the revenues and expenses shown on an income statement. As shown in the cash flow diagram (figure 8.2), cash can also be generated via loans and capital infusions and can be spent on assets, such as intangibles, equipment, debt payments, and investments. The following example illustrates how a transaction that would simply be an expense on an income statement is actually a generator of cash when accounted for on a cash flow statement.

A company purchases a piece of equipment that costs $10,000; it takes out a $7,000 loan to do so. The company then has $3,000 of cash invested in the equipment:

Cost:	$10,000
Less:	$7,000 loan
Cash In:	$3,000

The company then sells the equipment for $9,000, $1,000 less than the cost (ignoring depreciation). The income statement would then show a loss:

Sales Price:	$9,000
Cost:	$10,000
Profit (Loss):	($1,000)

But, while the income statement only shows the profit and loss of the situation, the cash flow statement shows how much *cash* was actually generated or lost; in this case, $2,000 was generated.

Cash Received:	$9,000
Loan:	$7,000
Cash Generated:	$2,000

From this example, it is clear that an income statement or balance sheet alone is insufficient to provide a complete financial assessment of a company. The cash flow statement fills in the details that the other two statements leave out.

Preparation and Structure of Cash Flow Statements

Every cash flow statement includes information in three categories that correspond to the three aforementioned components of cash in accounting:

- Funds from operations
- Financing activities
- Investing activities

Most companies work on a production-sales-collection cycle. That means they make something (or buy inventory), then sell it, and later collect payment from customers. The amount of cash required for a given cycle depends on three variables:

- The company's balance at the beginning of the cycle
- The length of the cycle
- How long the company can delay payment of its own payables

With these variables in mind, the purpose of the cash flow statement is to identify the change in working capital or cash from the prior period in order to verify that all sources and uses have been identified.

Note: Cash shortages, particularly during growth stages, are possible since the company is turning liquid assets (cash) into other types of assets such as inventory and accounts receivable, in order to support the growth. If the company is profitable, cash inflows will ultimately exceed cash outflows.

Figure 8.6 shows a sample cash flow statement. Where the income statement for the sample company ended with a net income figure of $1,369.48, the cash flow statement for the same company begins with that number. In terms of cash flow, the net income figure represents the starting source of cash as a summary of the revenue and expense tally from the income statement.

All of the items on a cash flow sheet are either *sources* or *uses* of cash:

- **Funds from operations.** Adjusts for any increases (sources) or decreases (uses) in net income that *does not* result in a flow of assets into or out of the business.
- **Financing activities.** Adjusts for transactions that impact either the long-term debt or the equity component of the sample company's balance sheet.
  » If there is an increase in financing activity, resulting, for example, from the sale of bonds or common stock, this is considered a source of cash and is added to the cash flow.
  » If there is a decrease resulting, for example, from the distribution of dividends (as with our sample company), it is considered a use of cash and is subtracted from the cash flow.
- **Investing activities.** Adjusts for transactions that specifically impact the non-current asset area of the sample company's balance sheet. For example, if long-term assets are sold, this is considered a source of cash and should be added to the cash flow. Conversely, if long-term assets are purchased with cash, this is a use of cash and should be subtracted from the cash flow.

A cash flow statement should answer the following questions:

- **Is money being generated through operations?** Cash flow generated by operations should be positive indicating that the company is fulfilling its mission.
- **Is money being reinvested in the company?** If cash flow is negative, it indicates that the company is buying assets faster than it is selling them. It is normal for start-ups and expanding companies to have a negative cash flow.

FIGURE 8.6 Sample cash flow statement

Vandelay Remodeling, LLC
Statement of Cash Flows
Current Period from 12/1/2010 to 12/31/2010, Year to Date from 1/1/2010 to

	Current Period	Year to Date
Operating Activities		
Net Income (loss)	-11,196.24	1,369.48
Adjustments to reconcile net income to net cash provided by operating activities		
Depreciation	4,500.00	4,500.00
Changes in operating assets & liabilities		
Accounts Receivable	-1,250.00	-51,250.00
Deposits	0.00	0.00
Inventory	0.00	0.00
Prepaid Expenses	0.00	0.00
Deposits & Escrows	0.00	0.00
Accounts Payable	8,500.00	8,799.85
Taxes Payable	0.00	0.00
Accrued Expenses	0.00	0.00
Total Cash used in operating activities	553.76	-36,580.67
Financing Activities		
Proceeds from Long Term Debt	0.00	0.00
Repayments of Long Term Debt	0.00	-2,000.00
Proceeds from Mortgages Payable	0.00	0.00
Repayment of Mortgages Payable	0.00	0.00
Proceeds from Capital Contributions	0.00	0.00
Distribution to Investors	0.00	0.00
Dividends	0.00	0.00
Adjustments to Retained Earnings	0.00	0.00
Net Cash Used in Financing Activities	0.00	-2,000.00
Investing Activities		
Purchase of Investments	0.00	0.00
Sales of Investments	0.00	0.00
Purchase of Property & Equipment	0.00	0.00
Sales of Property & Equipment	0.00	0.00
Purchase of Intangible Assets	0.00	0.00
Sales of Intangible Assets	0.00	0.00
Net Cash used in Investing Activities	0.00	0.00
Net Increase in Cash	553.76	-38,580.67
Beginning Cash	1,206.09	40,340.52
Ending Cash	1,759.85	1,759.85

Unaudited - For Management Purposes Only

- **Is money being generated through financing?** The answer to this question can be interpreted in different ways. For instance, a large amount of money coming in through financing might be an indicator that the company is expanding. Conversely, it could indicate that the company is desperate for cash and financing everything in sight.

Armed with what you have compiled from the three basic financial statements, your organization can now compare and correct. In these steps, the compiled information is analyzed and steps are taken toward improvement, as necessary.

Step 4—Compare

The next step is to compare your numbers to the plan. To stimulate and increase profit, a business must be monitored via comparison to historical data and/or industry comparables. As we discussed in the last chapter, this also includes comparing your expected break-even point to your actual break-even point. You should compare numbers in variance reports to locate "leaks" in the system.

Another common comparison is called ratio analysis, which is simply computing ratios relevant to your business and comparing them to historical data and industry data. The four major categories of ratios are:

- **Profitability ratios.** percentage of net profit to sales, percentage of gross margin to sales, percentage of various expenses to sales
- **Liquidity ratios.** acid ratio, current ratio, working capital, net worth to total assets
- **Turnover ratios.** inventory turnover, A/R and A/P turnover
- **Debt ratios.** debt to assets, debt to equity

You can take the analysis any number of steps further to compare you company's performance to other benchmarks. For example, return on investment analysis relates various ratios such as profitability and turnover to return on assets. Return on assets is then related to financial leverage to determine return on investment.

The bottom line is that whatever numbers you are comparing, you want to analyze variances between budget and actual figures, watch for unusual items in any statement, and large or unusual changes from one period to another. You also want to watch for trends, especially unfavorable, in comparative statements.

Take a look at the report shown in figure 8.7, comparing expected income statement with the actual income statement.

FIGURE 8.7 Comparing budgeted income statement with the actual

Vandelay Remodeling, LLC
Income Statement - Budget vs. Actual - Detail
Current Period from 12/1/2010 to 12/31/2010, Year to Date from 1/1/2010 to 12/31/2010

	Current Period			Year to Date		
	Actual	Budget	Variance	Actual	Budget	Variance
Income						
4100 - Sales	63,750.00	50,000.00	13,750.00	565,219.00	600,000.00	-34,781.00
Total Income	63,750.00	50,000.00	13,750.00	565,219.00	600,000.00	-34,781.00
Cost of Goods Sold						
5100 - Cost of Goods Sold	43,800.00	35,000.00	-8,800.00	422,273.00	420,000.00	-2,273.00
5101 - Supplies	8,500.00	0.00	-8,500.00	8,500.00	0.00	-8,500.00
Total Cost of Goods Sold	52,300.00	35,000.00	-17,300.00	430,773.00	420,000.00	-10,773.00
Gross Margin	11,450.00	15,000.00	-3,550.00	134,446.00	180,000.00	-45,554.00
General & Admin Expenses						
6010 - Salaries &Wages	0.00	1,750.00	1,750.00	26,250.00	21,000.00	-5,250.00
6020 - Salaries & Wages - Officers	0.00	5,291.67	5,291.67	55,000.00	63,500.04	8,500.04
6040 - Employer Taxes	0.00	750.00	750.00	8,635.00	9,000.00	365.00
6050 - Employee Benefits	0.00	333.33	333.33	3,978.00	3,999.96	21.96
6110 - Advertising	0.00	416.67	416.67	2,500.00	5,000.04	2,500.04
6150 - Auto Expenses	0.00	125.00	125.00	976.77	1,500.00	523.23
6160 - Bad Debts	0.00	41.67	41.67	348.75	500.04	151.29
6170 - Bank Fees	625.00	125.00	-500.00	625.00	1,500.00	875.00
6200 - Computer & Internet Expenses	0.00	125.00	125.00	1,603.00	1,500.00	-103.00
6230 - Depreciation	4,500.00	4,500.00	0.00	4,500.00	4,500.00	0.00
6280 - Insurance	0.00	375.00	375.00	3,000.00	4,500.00	1,500.00
6320 - Interest	0.00	125.00	125.00	2,500.00	1,500.00	-1,000.00
6330 - Legal & Professional	6,500.00	625.00	-5,875.00	6,500.00	7,500.00	1,000.00
6360 - Meals & Entertainment	1,700.00	158.33	-1,541.67	1,700.00	1,899.96	199.96
6370 - Office & Shop Expenses	0.00	250.00	250.00	1,299.85	3,000.00	1,700.15
6380 - Permits & Fees	0.00	83.33	83.33	295.00	999.96	704.96
6390 - Phone	0.00	200.00	200.00	2,567.32	2,400.00	-167.32
6400 - Postage & Freight	953.75	100.00	-853.75	953.75	1,200.00	246.25
6410 - Printing	0.00	125.00	125.00	1,476.59	1,500.00	23.41
6420 - Rent	7,500.00	625.00	-6,875.00	7,500.00	7,500.00	0.00
6430 - Repairs	867.49	83.33	-784.16	867.49	999.96	132.47
Marketing	0.00	0.00	0.00	0.00	0.00	0.00
Other Operating Expenses	0.00	0.00	0.00	0.00	0.00	0.00
Total General & Admin Expenses	22,646.24	16,208.33	-6,437.91	133,076.52	144,999.96	11,923.44
Net Operating Income (Loss)	-11,196.24	-1,208.33	-9,987.91	1,369.48	35,000.04	-33,630.56
Non-Operating Income & Expenses						
Other Operating Expenses	0.00	0.00	0.00	0.00	0.00	0.00
Total Non-Operating Income &	0.00	0.00	0.00	0.00	0.00	0.00
Net Income	-11,196.24	-1,208.33	-9,987.91	1,369.48	35,000.04	-33,630.56

Unaudited - For Management Purposes Only

Your comparison should answer the following questions:

- **Where do I have variances?**
- **Are the variances in this period greater than or less than the variances in the same item throughout the year to date?** If your variances are greater this period (in the negative), then something is wrong. If the variances are returning to zero, then things are back on track.

- **Do I have variances where I really shouldn't?** For example, why did I not budget for salaries, etc. this period? Is there something wrong with our budgeting process?
- **Can my bottom line profit or loss be attributed to a few specific variances?** Understanding where you went wrong (or right) helps plan for next period.

"A number in and of itself has no value."

This is a repeat! Now, I'm going to teach you the secret to being an accountant. A number in and of itself has no value. For instance, let's say I tell you that I earned $300,000 last year. Is that good or bad? Well, you have no way of knowing until I compare that to my earnings from the year before. For instance, if I earned $200,000 two years ago, then $300,000 is good. On the other hand, if I earned $2 million two years ago, then $300,000 is a crisis.

Thumbs up or thumbs down?

You need a benchmark, a number, to compare your current results to. Managing your business is nothing more complicated than comparing two numbers. If you have that, then you can say something is good or bad and requires attention. You don't need to be a mathematician; you just need to be able to point your thumbs. Thumbs up or thumbs down! With a basic understanding of your financial and operational dashboard, you are no longer flying blind.

Step 5—Correct

Problems are differences in expected results and can be good or bad. But acknowledge the difference and determine if you want to correct or ignore the situation. Solutions to get back on track are diverse, but let's take a logical method of approaching them.

Develop a Manageable Problem Solving Statement

This is essential if management wants to have a high probability of solving the problem. A manageable problem solving statement must include four key elements: (1) what the entity has in numeric terms, (2) what the entity wants in numeric terms, (3) a time frame, and (4) necessary constraints or parameters.

Create a problem-solving statement by describing the following items:

- What you have
- What you want

- What caused the problem
- Steps to solve the problem and
- Time frame

One format for a manageable problem-solving statement is:

To _____ from _____ to _____ by utilizing these steps _____

     (Objective)   (Current state)   (Goal)   (List steps)

by _____.

   (Date)

Or alternatively:

To _____ _____ from _____ to _____ by _____.

  (Increase/Decrease)   (Noun)   (Current state)   (Goal)   (Date)

For instance, suppose you want to decrease the collection cycle on accounts receivable from 90 days to 45 days. This goal would be hard to achieve in a one-year time frame, but interim goals could be to decrease the collection cycle by 15 days a year for each of the next three years. Our *problem solving statement* would be:

> *To reduce the collection cycle from 90 days to 45 days by changing*
> *our credit and collection policies as follows: (list steps). The goal would be*
> *accomplished over three years by lowering the collection cycle by*
> *15 days a year for each of the next three years.*

How can you use the income statement to correct the trajectory of your company?

To correct in financial management terms is to address variances in budgets or plans—differences in what was expected versus what actually happened. Some of the methods to address variances are listed below:

- Adjusting expenses
- Raising margins
- Revising projections
- Modifying estimating numbers if needed, so as to buy better

Here is just a sample of techniques to increase your profits:

- **Sales.** The goal of sales is to create a revenue stream that is predictable. Problems include: fictitious sales, unrecorded sales, bad inventory management, discounting, pricing problems. Solutions include: eliminate unprofitable products, departments, sales territories, add or delete options. Increased sales volume may require increasing the number of jobs or increasing the price of the jobs. Review your estimating procedures, consider greater geographic coverage and/or create better advertising programs to generate repeat business or referrals.

- **Cost of sales.** Obviously for each dollar of revenue you would like to minimize your out-of-pocket costs. Tools to lower your costs of sales may include better scheduling, better job-cost containment, getting better bids from vendors, eliminating jobs that do not have adequate profit margins, eliminate unprofitable products.

- **Gross margin.** Here the goal is to maintain consistency or better-than-average gross margins without sacrificing quality. Problems include: production procedures, quality issues, returns, training, high overhead costs, and management of factors of production. Solutions include: cut waste, work with vendors, manufacture the product faster, estimating procedures, standard costs systems, activity-based accounting, make or buy decisions, controlling indirect costs, managing marketing costs.

- **G&A costs.** Here the goal is also to spend enough to make the operations run smoothly but not more than necessary. You need to analyze the overhead such as salaries, staffing, benefits, insurance, interest, marketing, and sales commissions to make sure that these elements of your organization are in sync with your business plan. Don't forget to compare these items with your business plan.

How can you use the balance sheet to correct the trajectory of your company?

Remember that the income statement is only once facet of the big picture. Not only do you want to increase profitability, but also you want to increase cash flow. Analyzing your balance sheet does this. Here is just a sample of techniques to use to increase your financial wealth (the balance sheet). Some of the techniques may not pertain to your business but some of them will.

- **Cash.** The objective here is to minimize idle cash and still maintain liquidity. Problems include unpaid invoices, early payments by customers, money being generated or used for investments, suppliers demanding cash on delivery, theft, etc. Solutions: Consider doing better cash flow planning, tax planning, business planning, and budgeting. Also, do "what if" analysis to find out the consequences of your actions.

- **Accounts receivable.** The goal is to achieve an optimal balance between use of credit by customers and collecting receivables within a reasonable time to insure liquidity. Problems include: receivables not optimized due to collection efforts, sales, market use of credit, market segments, change in business climate, credit policies. Solutions include: managing A/R, reviewing credit and collection policies, and financing of receivables.
- **Inventories.** Since inventories are further removed from cash than receivables, the goal is to plan and gain control better. Consider managing inventory levels (specs versus pre-solds), review purchase decisions and review procedures and costs. Problems include: sales volume, stockpiling of goods, ordering procedures, buying practices, theft, spoiled or outmoded stock, fictitious purchases, reorder points missed, and stock outs. Solutions include: managing inventory levels, review purchasing decisions (estimating), procedures and costs, make scheduling and job costing an integral part of the way you conduct business.
- **Fixed assets.** The goal is to maximize utilization of plant and equipment. Problems include: wrong level of assets, extravagance, excess capacity, non-productive assets, and policies on modernization, leasing and expansion.
- **Current liabilities.** The goal is to use current debt as it relates to current assets and balance the two. Problems include: current debt levels, inventory levels, payment policies to vendors, unused trade discounts. Solutions include: managing trade credit, matching current liabilities to current assets (i.e., don't finance a long-term asset with short-term debt) and defer taxes and other payments.
- **Accrued expenses and taxes.** The goal is to defer taxes and other payments without sacrificing the liquidity of the company. When I say taxes, I am NOT talking about payroll taxes. Not paying these is usually a path to disaster.
- **Debt.** The goal is to maintain a debt level that does not hinder the cash flow and ultimately the profitability of the company. Problems include: rapid expansion, merger and acquisitions, heavy R & D industry, technological catch up, thinly capitalized, or too heavily capitalized. Manage debt by getting loans of a duration which match asset lives; don't borrow your overhead or lifestyle, use self–retiring debt.

Once again, the key to success is cash flow. Use all tools at your disposal to generate profits year after year and build your balance sheet so that more and more of it represents the owners' stake in the business.

Conclusion

Remember, profit is not created by accident. You need a solid idea of where you are going and how you are going to get there. Financial management entails not only the collection and presentation of information, but the *knowledge to interpret and act on that data.* Manage your business in the least amount of time necessary.

Understanding financial management is synonymous with being able to operate a successful business. Being able to work with the financial information that your company generates and to understand the trends that the numbers represent is crucial to making the decisions that distinguish highly successful organizations from lesser ones. Proper financial management entails not only the collection and presentation of information, but the knowledge and wherewithal to interpret and act upon that information.

Understanding the complexities and nuances of financial data is neither simple nor intuitive. And, because business owners have to worry about product development, construction, manufacturing, payroll, staffing and numerous other areas, financial management is often—albeit unintentionally—relegated to a lower priority. For many business owners, managing the company finances is little more than receiving a tax return.

Consulting an expert is a good way to give financial management the attention it deserves, and at the same time, benefit your company. The picture provided by a financial consultant enables more accurate planning for growth and profitability, and allows a company to adjust policies and procedures as needed to enhance cash flow. Perhaps most importantly, a skilled consultant eases the stress of financial management by arming a business owner with the tools needed to take growth and profitability to the next level.

Create Goals

To be successful in increasing positive cash flow you must:

_____ _____ from _____ to _____ by _____.
    (Verb)   (Noun)   (Number) (Number)   (Date)

Create Strategies

In order to meet this goal, you will:

_____ _____ by _____, _____, & _____.
   (Verb)   (Noun) by   (Action)   (Action) and (Action)

As an example, maybe after reviewing your financial statements, you discover that you don't have an appropriate level of liquid assets. A goal setting statement might be:

Increase current ratio from 0.91% to1.25% by June 2015.

Your strategy might be:

Increase cash flow from operations by controlling costs and billing customers earlier in the production cycle (including deposit and progress payments).

Once you've identified strategies (the "how you are going to achieve your goal"), it is time to create action plans. Action plans are a numbered list of required tasks. Each task has four components: task name, responsible party, due date, and completion status. Once you've completed your action plan, you should evaluate the strategy's costs, effectiveness, and return on investment.

How to Borrow Money

For nearly as long as humans have used money, humans have had banks. And through centuries of experience in lending money, banks have become very good at determining when a loan situation will benefit them; they know exactly what they're looking for. You notice I said, benefit *them*? That is the reality, even though banks often talk in terms of you, their customer. Therefore, you need to "groom" your banker/lender so they are more likely to accept your proposal or request.

This chapter is designed to provide a good overview of what all investors and lenders look for and how to present that information.

Getting Started

Although a loan package is typically made up of many complex financial documents, every package essentially addresses four basic questions:

- How much money does your business require?
- When does your business need the money?
- How will your business repay the investor?
- What is the risk associated with the loan?

Here lies one of the first differences between you as the business owner and the bank. For you, the first two questions are probably most important. After all, that's why you need to talk to the bank. You need to borrow a specific amount of money to do something. But which two questions are most important to the bank? The last two. So, before beginning to assemble the loan package, work out the answers to the following two questions:

- How will you pay back your investors?
- How will you demonstrate to investors that you can pay them back?

Steps in Raising Money

There really are just two main steps in raising money, which correspond directly to questions above. The first step is to determine how much you really need. This means identifying your cash needs *before you run out.* The second step is to prepare a loan request that speaks to the banker's needs, not yours. We'll discuss both steps in this process in detail below.

By now, you should be able to guess some of the ways you can determine how much is the right amount. Right? The amount of money you should ask for depends on many things, but in particular, your sales goals, overhead structure, cash-to-cash lifecycle (A/R and A/P), and capital expenditure needs (equipment, buildings, etc.). All things we've discussed in previous chapters. You also should know how you can identify your cash needs before you run out. Review your historical financial statements and create your business plan, *financial plan* (long-term cash flow), and budgets (short-term cash flow). Depending on your business, you should pay close attention to your sales schedule, overhead expense plan, and possibly your construction schedule and land development cost plan. You also should continuously review industry outlook and understand key factors that can impact your business.

After you know what you need, you need to understand how to approach a lender/investor. We'll discuss what the lender is looking for (including the 5 C's of credit), how to prepare a loan request, and review alternative sources of financing.

Cash Flow Projections

The cash forecast, projection, or proforma is a plan of cash receipts (money coming in) and cash expenditures (money going out) for a specific period of time, usually in monthly increments. As you know, cash is the lifeblood of a company. Cash flow forecasts should reflect the financial needs for operational requirements and *reserves for the unexpected.* If it reflects the operational needs, your operations people need to be involved in developing the forecasts. Too many companies think,

"Oh, that's the finance person's job." For some reason, they're always surprised when the forecasts are wrong and useless. And, for some reason, many of them never actually look at the forecasts. Instead, effective forecasting of your need for cash calls for an organized effort across your company, requiring the cooperation of the non-financial executives in particular.

By the way, a forecast is nothing more than an educated guess. The probability of a forecast being correct is negligible. So why do it? Because it becomes your benchmark.

This is important and can really make a huge difference in the success of your company. So let's reiterate a few points from earlier. If you have an effective cash flow forecast, you can spot problems *before they occur*. Forecasts provide a control or checkpoint useful in uncovering deviation from plans. By comparing deviations of forecasted levels of cash with actual results, management is offered an opportunity to revise or react to unforeseen or uncontrollable developments. In other words, you can identify potential cash shortfalls (warning signals) before they happen and take appropriate action, often for a fraction of the cost that it would require if you wait until they happen. In fact, a forecast can allow you to create a contingency plan in the event things don't happen as planned that is even less disruptive to your company.

Cash flow forecasts don't just prevent problems or lessen the impact once problems arise; they can help you grow your business as well in many ways. For example, you can ensure you have sufficient cash flow before you make a major financial commitment by knowing how much you have, what you need, and what you will need. You can identify when you have sufficient assets to take on additional business or when to consolidate your operations to maintain steady growth. I mentioned contingency plans (when things go wrong), but having a cash flow forecasts also lets you evaluate various options moving forward. By forecasting how they will impact cash flow, you can determine the financial feasibility of various programs before commitments are made. You also can put yourself in a better position to take advantage of cash discounts, make small-term investments, or take advantages of other opportunities to use liquid funds more profitably.

Having cash flow projections also provides intangible benefits, such as enabling you to keep staff, customers, and suppliers happy. It's a little known fact that people like to get paid. On time. This includes staff and suppliers. They also like to know they're going to get paid next week or next month without issues too. Customers are picky too. They want to know they can get the product or service they pay for on time (if not immediately). They don't want to hear that you're temporarily out of stock or unavailable (because you didn't forecast properly).

To recap, having effective cash flow forecasts helps prevents problems, helps you grow your company, and keeps everyone around you happier. What does that all mean? It means *you* will have a better life style.

Back to the focus of this chapter, yes, cash flow projections facilitate the raising of additional cash. They not only give the company advance warning in which to plan and develop sensible borrowing programs, but they also inspire confidence by the lenders in the firm's management. By presenting a cash flow schedule to your lender, he can help you determine your long-range borrowing needs. This does not mean that you obtain these funds before you need them, but it means that you will need to make proper arrangements so that the funds will be available to you when needed.

Creating a Cash Flow Projection

Now that we've hopefully convinced you that you need to create cash flow projections (if you need convincing), it's probably only fair that we show you how. None of this should be new at this point, because we are really just pulling together a lot of what we have done throughout this book.

Step 1. Establish your objectives. What do you want to do? For your business, this is done through the 7 Number analysis.

Step 2. Determine your cash inflows from sales. Start with a sales forecast (since sales are generally geared to the rate of sales activity). Previous sales volume is usually the springboard for sales predictions. This data should be related to other historical data, such as economic indicators, pricing policies, and competitive conditions. Also take into consideration your advertising and other promotion plans, seasonal variations, and production capacity. (Remember the chapter about fixed costs?) It is very important you don't work alone, in a vacuum. Work with your people to set quantifiable goals and get their commitment to reach those goals.

Step 3. Determine your cash outflows. Start with your costs of production and develop a production budget. I like to work in units first then dollars. When doing your cash flow forecast, use the internal build-up approach. How many units can you realistically deliver? Begin with how many lots are available already. Add in your production capacity and growth capabilities (organization strength). Factor in the anticipated market acceptance of the product and sales capacity. And consider the local lending climate for your customers—if they will need to borrow money to pay you. This all helps you determine how many units you can produce each month. Then, extend units to be produced by unit costs and drop that into your cash flow projection. Your production costs need to factor in the timing of disbursements (i.e., for a home you incur costs for six months before you finally sell it) as well as material usage and purchases, direct labor costs, and indirect variable costs.

Cash outflows also include overhead costs. They fall into three major categories:

- Fixed, such as property taxes, rent, interest on long-term indebtedness
- Semi-variable, which tend to be fixed based on a management decision (salaries, personnel costs, etc.)
- Variable, such as utilities, supervision, salespeople

Step 4. Determine what expenses you'll need to pay that aren't shown on your income statement, such as equipment and other capital expenditures, repayment of principal on loans, and dividends to shareholders (partners, investors, etc.).

Step 5. Determine when you will receive the draws from your lenders for the jobs, then include all other sources of cash of a routine nature (i.e., land sales, sale of warehouse, deposits, as well as loans or investments). After completing this step, you should have a good projection of your cash flow for every month looking out the next 12 months (if not farther).

Step 6. Measure performance and progress and help your people achieve their goals. To do this, look at cost/profit ratios, timeliness, and quantity of work done. These are all objective measures that are easy to quantify. But, you also need to measure quality, which sounds subjective, but can be quantified (often in terms of costs to repair or replace).

By analyzing your cash flow, you will be able to predict your seasonal fluctuations of cash. It should be noted that good reports can help reach conclusions within minutes. This doesn't require advanced degrees or hours of your time!

How to Approach a Lender/Investor

After you do the analysis and find that you do need additional money to either fund further investment in your company's growth or otherwise need to borrow money, it may be time to prepare yourself to meet with your lender or an investor. Let's talk about bankers first.

In general, banks and other lenders make their profit by renting money. In many regards, they are selling both a product and a service. The product is cash, and the service is the use of it for a specified period. On the individual level, loan officers are expected to sell loans and encourage customers like you to borrow. But the loan officer must become your advocate and convince the loan committee that you are a good risk. This sell is often much harder for them. So you need to get the loan officer on your side and convince them that you are a good risk. Keep in mind though, the banker must live with bank examiners. So, you have to help them look good in their colleagues' eyes. You do this by presenting appropriate information that is honest and well-put together.

What is the lender looking for?

This is a fundamental question, but one many business owners get wrong. Some people think the lenders are looking for companies that are going to have explosive growth in value. Others think the lenders are looking to help companies through tough times (i.e., touching stories, such as "Please. I need the money or else we will have to go out of business."). But the reality is that lenders are looking for low-risk investments in companies with sustainable profits. They also want to make loans that build a favorable image among certain groups and provide the most productive use of their capital.

Now let's review how to deliver this to them, starting with the loan package. Lenders want to see complete and well-prepared loan packages. Therefore, be ready to demonstrate the financial feasibility of both existing projects and new projects. Show them your company has healthy cash flow as well as good financial and operational management. Equity is important too, although not in the same way it is to investors. What is important to a lender is that the borrower (you) has enough business or personal capital to cover the remaining costs of the loan. After you receive the loan, you need to give regular updates on how you run your operations (make sure you communicate regularly with your money source).

Again, for you, the inability to adequately finance your business will result in less growth, lower profitability, or possible bankruptcy. For the lender, not financing your business will mean they'll finance the next business that meets their criteria. Your banker is interested in the following information:

- Importance of your loan to his/her bank
- Policies of his bank in terms of risk and where you fit in
- Loyalty of borrowing customers
- Amounts already invested by the bank in loans (availability of money)
- Other services the bank can provide you
- Availability of money to one borrower (in terms of the bank's limit on the size of loans)

- Economic and industry conditions
- Conditions imposed by the latest and greatest legislation
- Whether your methods of repayment fit their strategy:
  - » How much are you going to borrow?
  - » When will you repay the loan?
  - » How will you repay the loan?

Establishing Credibility to Establish Credit

No matter where you choose to seek financing, you will have to convince the lender/investor that you are a worthy risk. You need to establish your credibility by doing the following:

- **Demonstrating you're a good manager.** The proof is in the pudding, so this means showing the growth of your company and your ability as a cash flow engineer.
- **Showing evidence of careful planning and demonstrating that you compel events to conform to your plans.** This means having budgets and reviewing budget versus actual reports, the correcting as necessary.
- **Urging your banker to visit your company.** This builds trust and can demonstrate how well run the company is.
- **If your banker desires, obtaining audited financial statements.** An audited financial statement is a systematic examination of your financial statement where the end product is an opinion on the fairness of the presentation. In addition, some CPAs will give you a letter of recommendation, which will help you strengthen your system of internal control.

Thus, in order to establish a line of credit, you need to pin down arrangements in advance so you can hedge against unfavorable conditions and insure fund availability.

The 5C's of Credit

When a bank or investor evaluates the appeal of your company as an investment, they measure potential according to the 5 C's:

- **Character.** Your willingness to pay. It's a big picture assessment of both you and your company.

- **Capacity or capital.** Your cash flow and the fiscal strength (wealth) of your company.
- **Collateral.** Security for the loan—the assets pledged towards repayment of the loan.
- **Circumstances/Conditions.** An assessment of the economy, market, and industry influences.
- **Coverage.** Your company's insurance situation in case things go bad.

Addressing each of these in your loan request package greatly improves your chances of getting a loan. As you continue to read and think about your business needs, keep in mind the following questions:

- How does your business measure up to each of the 5 C's?
- What do you already have to assist in making your presentation?
- What additional information will you need to make your presentation?
- How will you present your business in the most attractive manner possible to an investor?
- What questions is an investor likely to ask about your business? Anticipating questions is an excellent way to show an investor that you've given careful thought to the loan process.

When considering the information you will present to a bank or investor, the importance of honesty cannot be underestimated; it is far worse to receive a loan under false pretenses than it is to give a less-than-perfect answer. Now let's dive into the 5 C's of credit.

1. Character

If you were lending money, you would surely want to know as much as you could about the person or organization making the request. Banks also want to know as much as they can. They want to know about your company, including its key players. They want to see honesty, integrity, and ability. They want to know if you have a good history or a less-than-stellar reputation. They want to know that you'll be accessible, responsive, and responsible in both success and failure. To illustrate personal and corporate character, a loan package should include the following:

An Introduction

- An overview of the company and what it does
- The company history

- The company's strengths and specialties
- Current holdings, employees, market positions, products, management qualifications, marketing, production, and market demographics
- What's ahead: company goals, objectives, and strategies; new markets, new technology, new production methods; jobs created. Address both the short and long term (over one year)
- Resumes of owners and key players

Three Years of Financial Documents

- Company financial statements (balance sheets, income statements, cash flow statements)
- Company tax returns
- Personal tax returns
- Current year to date financial statements
- Fair market value statements
- Appraisals
- Marketing plans
- Financial projections (forward-looking financial statements)
- Personal financial statements

Business Plan

A business plan is a blueprint for both your management team and your company's investors. It is a guide to how your company and its infrastructure will provide the goods or services it offers. The business plan is a qualitative description of the overall operation of your organization, and as such, can be thought of as describing the body of your company.

Financial Plan

If the business plan describes the body of your company, the financial plan can be thought of as the bone structure that supports the body. A solid financial plan shows that a company has a viable product and can produce enough revenues at low enough costs to support itself.

More specifically, while the business plan is qualitative, the financial plan is a quantitative estimate of how a company will operate in the future, and is used to do the following:

- Plan for strategic growth
- Create budgets

- Create benchmarks
- Improve coordination amongst employees and departments
- Improve cash management
- Provide a financial blueprint

Investors really like to see pictures—particularly in the building and real estate industries. So, after you've finished your introduction, be sure, when relevant, to include some pictures of your company's more impressive projects. For project-specific requests, include architectural renderings, pictures of models, photos of land to be developed, and any other pictures that might appeal to a potential investor.

2. Capital

The second C stands for capital, also referred to as capacity, and it represents the overall fiscal strength of a company. It is *not* about day-to-day finances. Rather, the capital section of your loan package describes a business's current capital situation, and how that business has handled capital in the past.

More specifically, the capital section uses ratio analysis to interpret the figures provided in the first section. If an investor provides your business with a loan, you need to demonstrate that the money will be used in a productive way. The ratios for any company should also be compared to industry-standard ratios: if the ratios for your business do not compare favorably to industry standards, you should be able to explain why there is a discrepancy *and* how your organization is taking steps to correct the situation.

In addition, the capital section should show the funds that are currently available to run your business. Don't worry that a lender will not write a loan if your business does not already have capital. Investors want an understanding of your company's long-term financial outlook. With small businesses, for example, banks are especially interested in how much money the owner has personally invested in the business—there is no greater illustration of how committed an owner is to the business's success.

To illustrate your capital situation, include the following items in the loan package:

- Indications of capital, internal strength, and track record
- Your averages and ratios, as compared to the industry (Industry-wide data is available from S&P and other organizations.)
  » Return on investment
  » Debt to equity ratios
  » Net profit as a percent of sales

>> Inventory turns
>> Asset turns
>> Any other ratios pertinent to your business and industry
- Amount of money in capital and retained earnings
- Cash flow statement (They'll also want to see it here to understand whether your current cash flow is from operating, investing, or financing activities.)

The reason this C is also called capacity is because you need to clearly show your capacity to pay the interest payments on time and pay back the principal when it is due. Common sources of repayment include:

- profits;
- sale of property;
- equity injection; and
- collateral.

3. Collateral

Investors naturally worry about what could happen if things go wrong. In detailing its collateral, a business shows potential investors that their money is safe even if the worst happens. The collateral section explains what assets are available to support the primary source of repayment, and if you are willing to commit personally invested funds, real estate, or inventory toward repayment.

The collateral section is an outline of the specific collateral a company holds, along with the values of each item. To determine your collateral offerings, check your financial statement to determine what qualifies as collateral and the financing available for the type of asset. For example, a bank doesn't count 100% of your inventory as collateral. Normally, only about 40–50% of the value of inventory can be applied toward collateral because a bank would have to sell the collateral—perhaps at a loss—and knows it will take time and resources to do so. The collateral section of a loan package should include *everything* that qualifies as collateral; the more assets shown, the more confident the investor. Table 9.1 illustrates many types of potential collateral

4. Circumstances

Every business has its own unique strengths and weaknesses that determine success or failure. Nevertheless, external influences are always present and must be accounted for in a loan package. It is important for the presentation to show an

TABLE 9.1 Types of collateral

Financing Asset	Financing Source	Amount Financed
Working capital	All sources	100%
Back-orders, contracts, purchase orders, work-in-process	Finance companies	80–100%
Receivables	Banks, factors	70–90%
Inventory	Banks, finance companies	40–50%
Equipment	Banks, leasing companies	70–100%
Leasehold improvements	Leasing companies	70–80%
Leases	Banks, finance companies, real estate lenders	50–80%
Real estate—commercial	Real estate lenders	70–90%
Real estate—residential	Real estate lenders	70–100%
Real estate—raw land and development	Real estate lenders	40–50%
Patents, trademarks and copyrights	Venture capital, strategic alliances, gov't programs	70–100%
Research and development	Venture capital, strategic alliances, gov't programs	70–100%
Success formula	Venture capital, strategic alliances, gov't programs	70–100%
Stocks, bonds, securities	All secured debt sources	60–80%
Collectibles	Venture capital, gov't programs, pawn brokers	70–100%

understanding of these influences and how they might affect your business. For instance, if the economy is in a recession, how will you maintain or grow your business? If the economy is inflationary, how will you keep up with the competition without having profits eroded by higher costs? What is the economic outlook for your city, your state, and your industry? With this in mind, the circumstances section of a loan package should present an assessment of current market conditions supported with data such as:

- Vacancy rates
- Employment rates
- Job growth
- Other pertinent statistics that apply to specific industries

This type of information is readily available from your local chamber of commerce, city and state sources, and other governmental agencies.

5. Coverage

The coverage section of a loan package describes insurance coverage on both the company itself and the key people in the organization. It should detail (including amounts and underwriters) all of the following:

- General perils insurance
- Liability insurance
- Life insurance
- Worker's compensation insurance
- Auto insurance
- Other insurance

Coverage also includes looking at the company's ability to meet financial obligations, repay the interest and the loan. It covers ratios like debt-to-equity, turnover ratios, utilization ratios and profit ratios.

Sources of Money

This chapter has centered on securing loans from banks. But small business owners are always surprised to know exactly how much money is available to them. There are many ways to generate capital, and they all fall into two categories:

- **Internal sources.** monies that can be raised through business operations, such as normal trade credit (buying something on account), customer advances, prepayments (including deposits), and accrued expenses and taxes (not payroll taxes). In addition, improved cash flow planning can help companies "discover" lost money or recover losses through better control. Owners' equity also can provide cash to the company; in fact, many owners put more equity into the company than they realize because they aren't taking a full salary.
- **External sources.** monies that can be raised through either debt (loans) or equity (ownership). This obviously includes bank debt, but other debt sources include lines of credit, letters of credit, insurance companies, pension plans, seller carrybacks, guaranteed loans, vendor financing, etc. Equity sources include equity partners, venture capital, joint ventures, partnerships, franchising, private and public offerings, or even selling to buyer. There also are hybrid-financing options like convertible bonds, preferred stock, etc.

Regardless of which source of capital you choose, every source will want to know the same things about their money. First, that it will be used wisely. Second, it will help them reach their objectives as much as it helps you achieve yours. And, last but certainly not least, that it will be given back plus whatever premiums they demand. So, you need to give them the information they need to make a decision:

- Financial statements for three years
- Tax returns (and know how they correlate to the financial statements)
- Projected income statements
- Projected cash flow statements

To really seal the deal, you need to give them answers *before* they ask the questions to show them that you are responsible, professional, and organized.

Conclusion

Finding the ideal financing source requires weighing many variables, such as how much money you need, when you need it, how you will pay it back, and the associated risk. But more than any single variable, it depends on the goals of the investor.

Investors don't just give money to anyone who asks. Whether it's a venture capitalist or a bank, the investor has a strategy and a focus; some invest only in small businesses, while others only invest in builders, and so on. With this in mind, understand that investors evaluate a business using their own investment criteria as well as a company's financial strength.

To successfully raise capital, you need to show how an investment in your company is a benefit to the investor as much as it is to you. So when you prepare your loan package, keep *their* criteria in mind, not just your needs. There are many ways to research the criteria and terms of the various sources of capital—consultants, industry organizations, the library, the Internet, the source itself. Be creative and be diligent; the more you learn about the source, the more you can tailor your loan package to their specific needs.

When you come in for a loan, remember that your banker sees your company different than you do. He is concerned with your profitability, financial records, your current financial strength, management ability, and your future plans. So be prepared to show him what he wants.

Create Goals

To be successful in securing a loan we must:

_____ _____ from _____ to _____ by _____.
    (Verb)   (Noun)   (Number) (Number)   (Date)

Create Strategies

In order to meet this goal, you will:

_____ _____ by _____, _____, & _____.
   (Verb)   (Noun)   by   (Action)   (Action)   and   (Action)

As an example, maybe after doing the analysis, you find that you need to increase revenue. A goal setting statement might be:

Increase monthly revenue from $100,000 to $150,000 by June 2015.

Your strategy might be:

Increase average price per transaction from $10,000 to $15,000 by focusing on value, not costs and by being more selective with customers.

Once you've identified strategies (the "how you are going to achieve your goal"), it is time to create action plans. Action plans are a numbered list of required tasks. Each task has four components: task name, responsible party, due date, and completion status.

Once you've completed your action plan, you should evaluate the strategy's costs, effectiveness, and return on investment.

10

Putting the 7 Key Numbers to Work for You

The key to effective sales and business management is to break them down into basic processes that are definable, measurable, manageable, consistent, and that deliver predictable results. Then, automate what can be automated and delegate what can be delegated. The objective is to free up your time and allow you to give attention to planning for the future, leading your team, and enjoying the fruits of success.

What is Integrated Management?

Integrated management is a process of managing technology and human input to get more done with less time, energy, or money invested. It is based on these principles:

- Understand clearly your goals and objectives.
- Monitor, manage, and measure your key metrics.
- Keep the most important thing, the most important thing.
- Develop processes that keep you and your employees focused and effective.
- Automate communications and processes where possible.

The 7 Key Numbers provide the framework that allows you to become an automated owner/manager. Having all the vital information you need available literally at a glance gives you the power to make immediate decisions to keep your business on target to reach your set goals without requiring you to spend hours poring over outdated reports that only show you part of the picture.

Managing Through Dashboards

As part of this process, you should be able to manage the key indicators of your business at a glance. Let's review three reports that you can use.

Cash flow

The first report is a summary of your financial situation. Create a dashboard or Excel spreadsheet that can track cash flow for your organization. Figure 10.1 is an example of cash flow presented using the Small Business Administration's (SBA) format. It shows beginning cash, sources of cash (both operating and non-operating such as debt and equity infusions) and uses of cash. Uses of cash include both operating and balance sheet uses. It then shows you your ending cash balance. This simple form is a thumbnail that helps determine if you are creating or destroying cash in your organization.

FIGURE 10.1 Cash flow using SBA format

	Month 1	Month 2	Month 3	Month 4	Month 5	Month 6	Month 7	Month 8	Month 9	Month 10	Month 11	Month 12
1. Cash on Hand	40,340.52	48,099.52	47,813.52	34,675.52	37,015.52	45,609.77	41,671.77	-5,513.23	-15,592.14	-6,172.14	742.86	1,206.09
2. Cash Receipts												
(a) Cash Sales	49,300.00	56,999.00	24,350.00	47,500.00	51,250.00	32,670.00	32,550.00	20,525.00	57,400.00	48,975.00	29,950.00	12,500.00
(b) Collections from Credit Accounts	0.00	0.00	0.00	0.00	0.00	0.00	0.00	0.00	0.00	0.00	0.00	50,000.00
(c) Loan or Other Cash Injection	0.00	0.00	0.00	0.00	0.00	0.00	0.00	0.00	0.00	0.00	0.00	0.00
3. Total Cash Receipts	49,300.00	56,999.00	24,350.00	47,500.00	51,250.00	32,670.00	32,550.00	20,525.00	57,400.00	48,975.00	29,950.00	62,500.00
4. Total Cash Available	89,640.52	105,098.52	72,163.52	82,175.52	88,265.52	78,279.77	74,221.77	15,011.77	41,807.86	42,802.86	30,692.86	63,706.09
5. Cash Paid Out												
(a) Purchases (Merchandise)	34,006.00	45,250.00	18,975.00	34,625.00	34,772.00	24,970.00	71,200.00	19,025.00	40,150.00	34,525.00	20,975.00	43,800.00
(b) Gross Wages (Excludes withdrawals)	6,750.00	6,750.00	13,750.00	6,750.00	6,750.00	6,750.00	6,750.00	6,750.00	6,750.00	6,750.00	6,750.00	0.00
(c) Payroll Expenses (Taxes, etc.)	785.00	785.00	4,763.00	785.00	785.00	785.00	785.00	785.00	785.00	785.00	785.00	0.00
(d) Outside Services	0.00	0.00	0.00	3,000.00	0.00	0.00	0.00	0.00	0.00	0.00	0.00	0.00
(e) Supplies (Office and operating)	0.00	0.00	0.00	0.00	0.00	1,603.00	1,000.00	0.00	0.00	0.00	0.00	0.00
(f) Repairs and Maintenance	0.00	0.00	0.00	0.00	0.00	0.00	0.00	0.00	0.00	0.00	0.00	867.49
(g) Advertising	0.00	0.00	0.00	0.00	0.00	2,500.00	0.00	0.00	0.00	0.00	0.00	0.00
(h) Auto, Delivery, and Travel	0.00	0.00	0.00	0.00	0.00	0.00	0.00	0.00	0.00	0.00	976.77	953.75
(i) Accounting & Legal	0.00	0.00	0.00	0.00	0.00	0.00	0.00	0.00	0.00	0.00	0.00	6,500.00
(j) Rent	0.00	0.00	0.00	0.00	0.00	0.00	0.00	0.00	0.00	0.00	0.00	7,500.00
(k) Telephone	0.00	0.00	0.00	0.00	0.00	0.00	0.00	2,567.32	0.00	0.00	0.00	0.00
(l) Utilities	0.00	0.00	0.00	0.00	0.00	0.00	0.00	0.00	0.00	0.00	0.00	0.00
(m) Insurance	0.00	0.00	0.00	0.00	0.00	0.00	0.00	0.00	0.00	0.00	0.00	0.00
(n) Taxes (Real estate, etc.)	0.00	0.00	0.00	0.00	0.00	0.00	0.00	0.00	0.00	0.00	0.00	0.00
(o) Interest	0.00	2,500.00	0.00	0.00	0.00	0.00	0.00	0.00	0.00	0.00	0.00	0.00
(p) Other Expenses												
(p1)	0.00	0.00	0.00	0.00	0.00	0.00	0.00	1,476.59	0.00	0.00	0.00	625.00
(p2)	0.00	0.00	0.00	0.00	0.00	0.00	0.00	0.00	0.00	0.00	0.00	0.00
(p3)	0.00	0.00	0.00	0.00	0.00	0.00	0.00	0.00	0.00	0.00	0.00	1,700.00
(p4)	0.00	0.00	0.00	0.00	0.00	0.00	0.00	0.00	0.00	0.00	0.00	0.00
(p5)	0.00	0.00	0.00	0.00	0.00	0.00	0.00	0.00	295.00	0.00	0.00	0.00
(q) Miscellaneous	0.00	0.00	0.00	0.00	348.75	0.00	0.00	0.00	0.00	0.00	0.00	0.00
(r) Subtotal	41,541.00	55,285.00	37,488.00	45,160.00	42,655.75	36,608.00	79,735.00	30,603.91	47,980.00	42,060.00	29,486.77	61,946.24
(s) Loan Principal Payment	0.00	2,000.00	0.00	0.00	0.00	0.00	0.00	0.00	0.00	0.00	0.00	0.00
(t) Capital Purchases	0.00	0.00	0.00	0.00	0.00	0.00	0.00	0.00	0.00	0.00	0.00	0.00
(u) Other Start-up Costs	0.00	0.00	0.00	0.00	0.00	0.00	0.00	0.00	0.00	0.00	0.00	0.00
(v) Reserve and/or Escrow	0.00	0.00	0.00	0.00	0.00	0.00	0.00	0.00	0.00	0.00	0.00	0.00
(w) Owners Withdrawal	0.00	0.00	0.00	0.00	0.00	0.00	0.00	0.00	0.00	0.00	0.00	0.00
6. Total Cash Paid Out	41,541.00	57,285.00	37,488.00	45,160.00	42,655.75	36,608.00	79,735.00	30,603.91	47,980.00	42,060.00	29,486.77	61,946.24
7. Cash Position	48,099.52	47,813.52	34,675.52	37,015.52	45,609.77	41,671.77	-5,513.23	-15,592.14	-6,172.14	742.86	1,206.09	1,759.85

It shows beginning cash, sources of cash (both operating and non-operating such as debt and equity infusions) and uses of cash. Uses of cash includes both operating and balance sheet uses. It then shows you your ending cash balance. This simple form is a thumbnail forms that helps determine if you are creating or destroying cash in your organization.

The 7 Key Number Dashboard

See how your whole system is running together—from lead generation to cash in the bank. Now we'd like to introduce you to our biggest game changer: a worksheet to show you your 7 numbers and predict cash flow.

If you don't have an automated system, you can still create this worksheet in Microsoft® Excel. I suggest using four columns: the first is the current month activity, the second is the year-to-date activity, the third is the scenario we choose to compare our data with (your ideal 7 Key Numbers you came up with in Chapter 1), and the fourth column is used to proactively model additional scenarios (fig 10.2). You can use this format to monitor trends by comparing your current period to your year-to-date or any other date range you choose. In this case, if you focus on

FIGURE 10.2 7 Key Number report

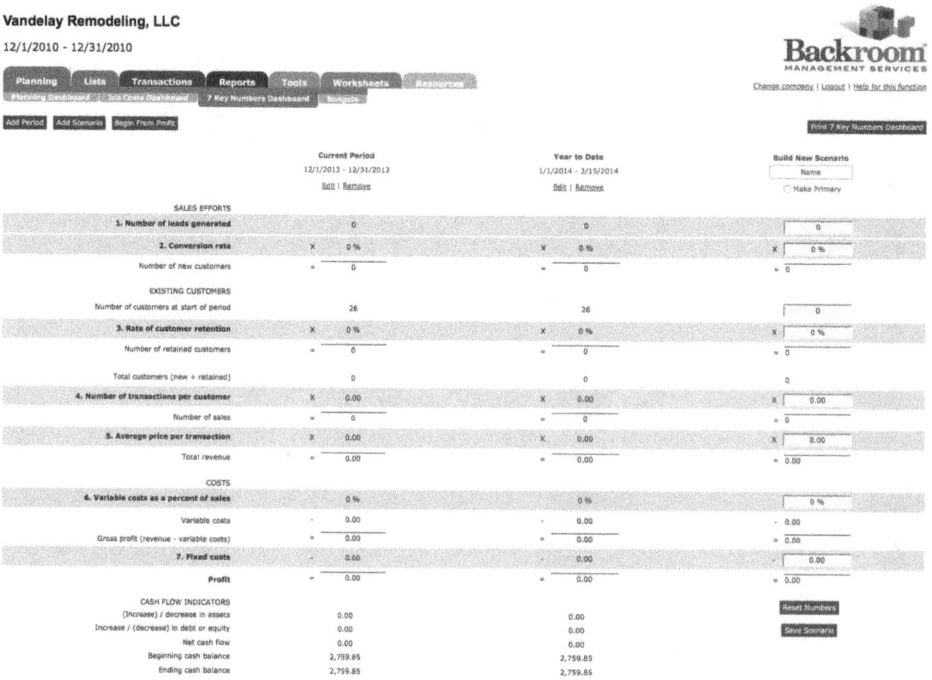

	Current Period 12/1/2013 - 12/31/2013 Edit | Remove	Year to Date 1/1/2014 - 3/15/2014 Edit | Remove	Build New Scenario Name Make Primary
SALES EFFORTS			
1. Number of leads generated	0	0	0
2. Conversion rate	X 0 %	X 0 %	X 0 %
Number of new customers	= 0	= 0	= 0
EXISTING CUSTOMERS			
Number of customers at start of period	26	26	0
3. Rate of customer retention	X 0 %	X 0 %	X 0 %
Number of retained customers	= 0	= 0	= 0
Total customers (new + retained)	0	0	0
4. Number of transactions per customer	X 0.00	X 0.00	X 0.00
Number of sales	= 0	= 0	= 0
5. Average price per transaction	X 0.00	X 0.00	X 0.00
Total revenue	= 0.00	= 0.00	= 0.00
COSTS			
6. Variable costs as a percent of sales	0 %	0 %	0 %
Variable costs	- 0.00	- 0.00	- 0.00
Gross profit (revenue - variable costs)	= 0.00	= 0.00	= 0.00
7. Fixed costs	- 0.00	- 0.00	- 0.00
Profit	= 0.00	= 0.00	= 0.00
CASH FLOW INDICATORS			
(Increase) / decrease in assets	0.00	0.00	
Increase / (decrease) in debt or equity	0.00	0.00	
Net cash flow	0.00	0.00	
Beginning cash balance	2,759.85	2,759.85	
Ending cash balance	2,759.85	2,759.85	

costs of goods sold, you can see that this month variable costs as a percent of sales are 82% compared to the yearly trend of 76%. The cost is going up, and that is creating a bad trend.

If you look at the year-to-date numbers compared to the ideal numbers, you can see the company is not hitting its profit margins, not hitting its pricing, and frankly, not hitting very many of its targets.

In the last column, this company can model their path and ask, "What if I hit my conversion rate? What if I can incrementally correct my pricing? What if I can control my costs? What if I did not try to correct all my problems in one fell swoop, but started getting my business back on track one step at a time (or, one Key Number at a time)?" And you can see the profit you're leaving on the table compared to where they are today.

Finally, a lot of owners ask, "Why is my profit different than my bank account?" Your worksheet will show you why cash and profit are not the same. This is why the 7 Key Numbers are so crucial. You need to track leading as well as lagging indicators. For instance, job profitability, before the job is done; time management, before you're paying your people more than the income potential of the engagement.

Remember, your goal is to generate more cash flow, and this system helps you get there faster. We also believe that management and accounting systems should help drive revenue and serve as an investment instead of a cost.

Job Profitability

The job-costs spreadsheets allow you to focus on your projected profit and cash flow from each and every job in real time. You can look at one job, a group of jobs, or all your jobs at once. Are your expected billings (revenue) greater than your costs? Have you billed more to date or incurred more costs to date? What is the expected cost to complete? You can summarize your jobs with the following information:

- Job name
- Estimated billings
- Estimated costs
- Variance
- Cash collected
- Cash paid out
- The difference between cash collected and cash paid out
- Unpaid bills
- Invoiced and not collected

- Projected overage or shortfall
- Balance left to bill customers
- Balance left to pay vendors

You can create two pie charts that allow you to compare your estimated profitability to your actual at a glance (fig 10.3). If the actual "slice" is smaller than the estimated, you know something is off track. You can then look at the table to dive down into the details.

FIGURE 10.3 Job-cost dashboard pie charts

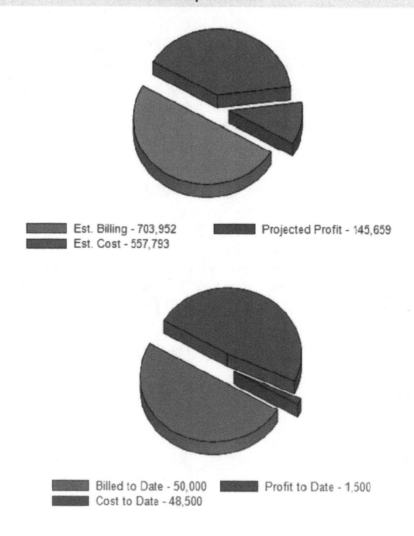

Est. Billing - 703,952   Projected Profit - 145,659
Est. Cost - 557,793

Billed to Date - 50,000   Profit to Date - 1,500
Cost to Date - 48,500

Final Conclusion

Here is the reality of running a business: most business owners assume that hard work and long hours are what he/she needs to become successful. But the problem is that hard work leaves you no time or energy to work *smarter*.

Our question isn't, "Are you working *on* your business?" but "Are you enjoying the benefits of owning a business?" Let's face it, as a business owner you only have three resources: time, energy, and money. But, here's the trap: you can spend your time doing things that add little value to the business, or develop systems and procedures that give you more time and create the flexibility of making more money (not just saving money).

Watching your numbers will give you the flexibility to pay yourself and your employees more, invest in marketing and advertising, and grow your business.

A lesson that I learned from one of my partners was: "If you take care of your business, your business will take care of you!" It's time to quit spinning your wheels and get off the treadmill. You have a choice: you can work on your business or be on top of your business and cash flow engineering. Again a set of simple sequential steps is the key to your freedom.

Imagine you're making an extra $5,000, $10,000, or $20,000 a month. Now multiply that by five or 10 years. Imagine how much money you are leaving on the table. What would be different for you in your life? I want you to imagine that right now. Would you be able to completely get out of debt? Would you be able to go on a great vacation with your spouse? Would you be able to start (and fill) that college fund for your kids? Would you be facing a nice retirement?

At the end of the day, when you're managing a business, increasing sales, or creating cash flow, you have to know how to track all your important numbers. You have to know what to look for, when to look for it, how to use the information, and what the limitations are, so that you can win. These are all skills that you have to have to be successful; fortunately, you can learn these skills!

We didn't have any when we first started; we had to develop them and we went on to be very successful without business ventures. We look forward to seeing you succeed!

Notes

1. A Joint Study from the National Association of REALTORS® and Google, "Digital House Hunt: Consumer and Market Trends in Real Estate," January 16, 2013, www.realtor.org/reports/digital-house-hunt.

2. Jack White, *The Messages of Effusion* (Corsicana, TX: Senkarik Publishing, 2005), 32, http://tinyurl.com/pzf7dk4.

3. Brianne Shelley, "How to Make Sure Your Website Passes the Dreaded Blink," *The Hubspot* (blog), January 18, 2013, http://blog.hubspot.com/blog/tabid/6307/bid/34061/How-to-Make-Sure-Your-Website-Passes-the-Dreaded-Blink-Test.aspx.

4. William "Skip" Miller, *ProActive Selling: Control the Process—Win the Sale, Second Edition,* (New York: AMACOM, 2012), 8, http://tinyurl.com/o3rbu7x.

5. "Why Consistent Follow Up Equals Sales Success, *Mind Capture Group* (blog), July 8, 2009, http://www.mindcapture group.com/blog/index.php?entry=entry090708-065644.

6. Jordie van Rijn, "The Ultimate Marketing Automation Statistics Overview" last updated December 2014, www.email monday.com/marketing-automation-statistics-overview.

7. A Joint Study from the National Association of REALTORS® and Google, "Digital House Hunt: Consumer and Market Trends in Real Estate," January 16, 2013, www.realtor.org/reports/digital-house-hunt.

8. Inc. Staff, "Converting Web Traffic into Sales Leads," *Inc.com,* December 1, 2009. www.inc.com/magazine/20091201/converting-web-traffic-into-sales-leads.html.

9. "Lead Response Management Study," *LeadResponseManagement.org,* 2009, http://www.leadresponsemanagement.org/lrm_study.

10. "Why Consistent Follow Up Equals Sales Success, *Mind Capture Group* (blog), July 8, 2009, http://www.mindcapturegroup.com/blog/index.php?entry=entry090708-065644.

11. Inc. Staff, "Converting Web Traffic into Sales Leads," *Inc.com,* December 1, 2009, www.inc.com/magazine/20091201/converting-web-traffic-into-sales-leads.html.

12. Inc. Staff, "Converting Web Traffic into Sales Leads," *Inc.com,* December 1, 2009, www.inc.com/magazine/20091201/converting-web-traffic-into-sales-leads.html.

13. Ian Michiels et al., "The Definitive Guide to Lead Nurturing," Marketo, Inc., 2009, https://www.marketo.com/_assets/uploads/definitive-guide-to-lead-nurturing.pdf?20130113032414.

14. Peter Valdes-Dapena, "Average U.S. car is 11.4 years old, a record high," *CNN.com,* August 6, 2013, http://money.cnn.com/2013/08/06/autos/age-of-cars.

Glossary

5 C's of financial management. These relate to your action plan and represent a proactive philosophy designed to continually sharpen and refine every one of your business processes. They are create, collect, compile, compare and correct.

5 C's of credit. When a bank or investor evaluates the appeal of your company as an investment, they measure your potential according to: character, capacity or capital, collateral, circumstances/conditions and coverage.

7 Key Numbers. Seven numbers that track your whole business funnel from lead generation to cash in the bank.

8 P's. A method to describe a business and drive strategies for change. They are: purpose, product, place, price, promotion, production, people (management), and profit (finance).

ABC approach to marketing. A marketing strategy to generate sales.

accrual basis. A method of accounting where transactions are recorded when they are incurred, regardless of whether cash has changed hands.

Arithmophobia. The fear of numbers.

assets. Things you own, although not necessarily paid for. They can be usually current or long-term.

balance sheet. A financial statement that gives a snapshot of the company's financial status at a given moment in time. It shows the assets, liabilities and equity.

benchmark. A number to which you compare your results

break-even analysis. A mathematical process for determining you break-even point. It can also be used as a management tool to determine additional revenues required to cover new expenses or profit goals.

break-even point. The point where total revenues equal total expenses.

break-even quantity. The number of units necessary to be sold given a certain profit margin.

budget. A process of estimating revenues and expenses before they occur.

budget administration. The process of comparing actual results to budgeted results.

business. A well-positioned, well-defined organization generating cash flow that encourages growth and leads to building wealth.

business plan. A blueprint for both your management team and your company's investors. It is a guide to how your company and its infrastructure will provide the goods or services it offers. The business plan is a qualitative description of the overall operation of your organization.

cash basis. A method of accounting where cash is accounted for when it is received and expenditures recorded when they are paid.

cash flow engineering. A process to ensure consistent and predictable cash flow. It integrates information, strategies and automation.

cash flow projection. A plan of cash receipts and cash expenditures for a specific period of time, usually in monthly increments.

cash flow statement. A financial statement that shows how changes in the balance sheet and income statement affected cash. This normally is presented in terms of operating, investing and financing activities.

conversion rate. The percentage of leads and/or prospects that become customers.

cost of goods sold (COGS, also cost of sales). Costs incurred to produce and sell the products that are recognized as sales in your income statement. (*see also* variable costs)

current assets. Assets that will be transformed into cash or used within one year.

current liabilities. Claims against a company that will be satisfied within a year.

customer lifetime value (CLV). The cumulative sum of every transaction stemming from a single buyer.

customer relationship management (CRM). A system for managing a company's interactions with its current and potential customers.

customer retention. A company's strategy to continue relationships with its current and potential customers for future sales.

customer value proposition (CVP). Your customer's belief in the value to them. *Their* return on engagement.

dashboards. A quick summary of key components of your business. The summary can be key numbers or graphical presentations of data.

elevator speech. Description of the benefits your company offers in 30 seconds or less.

equity. The value of a business to its owners after all obligations have been met. (*see also* net worth)

financial plan. A quantitative estimate of how a company will operate in the future.

financial statements. Documents that present the financial activities of a business; traditionally a balance sheet, profit and loss statement, and a statement of cash flows.

fixed costs. Costs that typically don't change from accounting period to accounting period and will occur whether or not you have any jobs. (*see also* overhead)

GAAP. Generally accepted accounting principles

gross margin/gross profit. The difference between revenue and costs of goods sold (before operating costs). This is stated in absolute dollars.

gross profit percentage. A ratio of gross margin divided by gross sales. It is expressed as a percentage.

ideal sales price. The price that exactly covers your costs of production, sales and other costs based on price and meets your gross profit goal.

income statement. A financial statement showing how much money a company is making or losing over a given time period.

integrated management. A process of managing technology and human input to get more done with less time, energy, or money invested.

lead. Prospective customers who have shown interest in your company, by clicking a link in an ad or filling out a form for more information.

lead magnet. Enticements to potential customers to get them to take action (e.g., express interest, request information) and convert them to leads.

lead nurturing. A system of communicating to a potential customer in a consistent and meaningful way.

liabilities. Obligations a company owes to outside parties.

long-term assets. Assets that will not be consumed or turned into cash within one year. (e.g., property, equipment, long-term investments)

long-term debt. Debts that are outstanding for more than a year or the normal operating cycle. (e.g., mortgages and bonds payable)

management by exception. A management technique where you spend time looking at significant deviations from your benchmarks and determining a course of action (if any) necessary to correct that deviation.

management by objective. A management technique where objectives are established, quantified, and then broken down into sub-goals (standards of performance).

marketing. The process of identifying and attracting qualified customers.

marketing message. A communication that engages your target market with a clear, relevant, compelling statement that includes a strong 'call to action' or incentive to take the next step.

marketing ROI. Return on investment for your marketing dollars.

marketing vehicle. A tool to deliver your marketing message to a specific audience. (e.g., website, newspaper ad, television ad)

markup. The difference between the cost of manufacturing a product and its sale price.

net worth. Total assets minus total liabilities of a company.

operating expenses. All expenses realated to the sale of merchandise or services plus all other costs related to operating the business.

optimal pricing. The ideal sales price adjusted to reflect management's pricing objectives.

overhead. Costs that typically don't change from accounting period to accounting period and will occur whether or not you have any jobs. (see also fixed costs)

pay-per-click (PPC). Paid search advertising that allows you to pay only for leads that click through your ad (versus those who see it but don't take action)

perfect cash flow cycle. A system that shows you how cash flows through your company and teaches you to spot trends in time to take corrective action if necessary.

problem solving statement. A concise statement outlining a description of issues that need to be addressed. It must include four key elements: 1) what the entity has in numeric terms, 2) what the entity wants in numeric terms, 3) a time frame to solve the problem, and 4) necessary constraints or parameters.

production cycle approach to pricing. Taking inventory of all the steps in production and the related cash outflows and matching them to your cash inflows.

profit and loss statement. An income statement showing how much money a company is making or losing over a given time period.

prospects. Potential customers who have shown serious interest in purchasing your product.

referral sales. When a previous or existing customer provides the name and contact information of a potential customer.

relevant range. A minimum and maximum level of production that can be achieved with a given overhead structure.

return on investment (ROI). The ratio of money gained or lost on an investment relative to the amount of money invested.

search corridor. All the places a buyer is likely to look for a solution like yours. (e.g., Google searches, newspaper, radio, TV, social media, word of mouth)

search engine optimization (SEO). Optimizing a website with specific keywords for greater visibility on search engines.

three key disciplines of a business. Sales and marketing, operations and finance.

unique selling proposition (USP). Tells prospective customers what is different about you, while still including the "what's in it for me?" message.

upsell. Enticing a customer to buy a more expensive product or a related additional product.

variable costs. Direct costs incurred to produce a product or service.

Index